C000072301

A Buzz in the Building

How to build and lead a brilliant organisation

Kate Mercer

A Buzz in the Building
How to build and lead a brilliant organisation
© Kate Mercer
ISBN 978-1-909116-56-6
eISBN 978-1-909116-57-3

Published in 2016 by SRA Books

The right of Kate Mercer to be identified as the author
of this work has been asserted by her in accordance with the
Copyright, Designs and Patents Act 1988.

A CIP record of this book is available from the British Library.

All rights reserved. No part of this book may be reproduced, stored
in a retrieval system, or transmitted in any form or by any means,
electronic, mechanical, photocopying, recording or otherwise,
without the prior written permission of the copyright holder.

No responsibility for loss occasioned to any person acting or
refraining from action as a result of any material in this publication
can be accepted by the author or publisher.

Illustrations © Stuart Roper
www.milagrodesign.com

Printed in the UK by TJ International, Padstow.

Contents

Introduction – Why this book right now?

In my more recent work as a consultant to large and small organisations, I've made a surprising observation: leaders are lacking a level in their skills.

How can this be? Surely there's no shortage of information and role models for great leadership? True, over the last 30 years or so a huge amount has been written about leadership, the qualities of leaders and the importance of having a vision, backed up by a set of personal and organisational values.

And it seems this message has largely been heard. I meet people at the top of large and small organisations with vision, with strong values and with their hearts in the right place.

They know how to run their business: how to make and deliver their product or service, how to market it, control their finances and stay the right side of the law. And they do care about people and their experience of working in the organisation – but many seem to have very little idea about how the organisation itself actually works and how to be its leader.

What they seem to have missed out on is working communication and organisational management skills: how to set up and, crucially, maintain teams of people who know where their leadership is taking the organisation. It takes skill to run an organisation in which the people who work in it happily take ownership of and accountability for the tasks of running the organisation, and remain enthusiastic, engaged and motivated to do their best.

These are the kinds of things people say when I begin to work with them:
- 'Why can't I get people to do what I want them to do?'
- 'No one shows any initiative.'
- 'Why do I have to do everything myself?'
- 'There's no enthusiasm, no buzz around here.'

Why this might be

It used to be that you served your time in growing organisations, gaining experience at each level before moving to the next. A lot of time, money and energy were spent on ensuring that you rounded out, not just your technical skills and your professional area of expertise, but also your supervisory, managerial and communication skills.

This has not been so much the case in recent years. Organisations are leaner and flatter, times have been hard and many have had to fight to survive. If you run your own business or you are employed by anything but a very large organisation, you may not have had the chance to go on training courses. Your focus has had to be on maintaining and developing technical and professional skills above every other priority, on retaining the best people and on parting company with those who aren't absolutely essential to the future of the business.

This has often led to the survival of high quality leaders with outstanding technical ability and insight, and with drive, vision and determination. It's even led to businesses that are lean, efficient and by some measures, very successful. But somewhere along the way, the 'soft' skills got lost. What I'm frequently seeing in my work is frustrated leaders and confused, demotivated employees who have an uneasy feeling that there must be more to organisational life than just financial and reputational success. Without a leader who has the skills to manage the development of the organisation as it grows, it becomes an unhealthy place to work, and the people in it are unhappy and fail to thrive.

How soft are soft skills?

Of course, though they are often called soft skills, there is nothing soft about them. The skills you need to create a great team, to engage people so they pour their enthusiasm and skills into making the operation a success, to build an *organisation* that is as successful as the *business* it supports, that customers want to work with and new employees want to come and be part of – these aren't soft skills, they are the ones that make organisational life worth living.

Who this book is for

If you've ever set up a business (or founded a charity, or started a group for some purpose), or risen to the top of your own particular bit of the tree, and have discovered, at some point, usually quite early on, that something seems to have gone wrong, this book is written for you.

Your company, your division, your group seems to have got away from you. It doesn't always do what you want it to do. The people working in it have developed ideas of their own and ways of doing things that you would never have thought of yourself. A little-known or understood fact about organisations is that they do suddenly 'come to life'. It happens very early on, and can happen when only two or three people come together. Sometimes this plays into your hands – other people's ideas are better than yours, or they like doing the things you don't. But this is a chance outcome – one that happens more by luck than judgement.

More often, your business, or your bit of it, arrives at a point where it seems to be going in a direction you didn't bargain on. You started it because you had a good idea, a great invention, a new service you wanted to make available to the world. Or you wanted the freedom and autonomy of running your own show. The day you started on this path, all things seemed possible – a future of freedom, self-expression and enjoyment seemed to open up in front of you.

But you've looked up a couple of years later and realised you're working harder than ever and it's not all enjoyable. Maybe you've thought, 'I didn't sign up for this. I signed up for freedom and self-expression and fun, and what have I got? I've got backbiting and firefighting, finger pointing and juggling. And, possibly worst of all, I've got people to manage. I'm just an engineer/a financial adviser/property specialist/a computer geek (fill in the blank yourself) – I don't have the skills to handle this bit. It's just too hard.'

So this book was conceived. Because the right way for you may or may not be to go forward from this point, to move into higher management or to allow your organisation to grow into a bigger one. It's true – you might be happier going back to being the specialist you once were or running a smaller organisation.

But wouldn't it be great to make that decision having explored what's possible in growing an organisation that supports and delivers your original business vision? Not to give up and retire defeated because it's all too hard, but to learn a thing or two about how organisations work when they suddenly acquire a life of their own? What skills might you need (or already have, but just aren't deploying)?

If you then decide not to go forward, at least you will have made the choice in the full knowledge of all the facts and consequences, rather than retiring hurt because you don't feel you are up to it.

Mindsets and skills

This book works by giving you a chance to explore and, if necessary, alter your own state of mind – your mindset – in respect of various aspects of your business. That's because it's incredibly important to make sure your heart and mind are in the right place before deploying 'tips and tricks' on people. Do this and you'll very quickly alienate them – you'll have a riot on your hands. People don't like being fixed. They don't like being regarded as a problem. And they don't like being *made* to do anything.

This book is going to explore two sets of factors.

First *mindsets*: those attitudes, values, and beliefs that got you to where you are today. An understanding of your own mindsets and the behaviours they give rise to will shed a useful light on what is happening around you and why. Understanding how your own mechanism works will give you an insight into how mindsets – yours and others' – give rise to unexamined assumptions about the way organisations work and shape people's motivations and behaviour.

These insights will help you see how things got to be the way they are in your organisation. You'll also be able to see what needs to change to allow all of you to understand each other and work well together. Together, you can explore the unexamined assumptions that cause misunderstandings and communication breakdowns. Then you can consciously create new mutual ways of looking at things that will make your relationships at work, and organisational life in general, a great deal easier. Understanding mindsets puts your hands on the controls of what's going on and makes leading your organisation less of a mystery.

Secondly, we'll look at *skills*. It's very likely that you have great technical skills, and quite possibly great social skills. But do you consciously have the working communication skills in place that you will need to run your organisation, and to create and maintain the change it will undergo as it grows? Possibly not. And you can't run a good organisation on technical skills and social skills alone.

Each chapter will first focus on a specific mindset – those you and others may already have that are causing the problem or holding you back from finding a solution, and new ones that will actively help you to lead your organisation and to coach others to be able to support you in your leadership. We'll deal with mindsets first, because you can't change your or anyone else's behaviour without a change in your, and their, mindset.

In the chapter following the exploration of each mindset, we'll explore one of the skills that the new mindset makes possible. In fact, you and others are very likely to have some or all of these skills already and will simply need to explore for yourselves how to use them effectively at work. If not, the skills you will need are not hard to learn, once the appropriate mindset is in place.

Each chapter in this book, whether mindset or skill, can be read in isolation – look at the chapter headings to see which to read if you have a specific issue or complaint about what's happening right now. But the chapters also form a journey, with each mindset shift informing and easing your passage to the next – if you are so inclined you might want to read the book in order, from beginning to end. You'll find a summary of the journey in the final chapter.

Whichever route you take, the mindsets and skills you learn will be useful not just at work but in other aspects of your life too: life skills for leaders, if you like.

Until you make the unconscious conscious,
it will direct your life and you will call it fate.

Carl Jung

In order to gain the most from this book, it is important to understand that there are some things you don't know – and you don't even know yet that you don't know.

There are also some things you know and can do that you do completely naturally and unconsciously: you are totally unaware of how skilled you actually are.

The material in this book is not rocket science. Much of it you will already have encountered in the course of your life and work. It may even be that you are struggling with something in your role as a leader at work, when you are actually very competent at exactly the same skill in a different environment. I see this sometimes with new leaders who feel they are too unconfident to assert their authority at work, yet who (for example) cheerfully manage and keep in perfect order a team of large and scary rugby players every weekend.

How can this be? How is it that you are sometimes completely unaware of a lack in your skills, either because you just don't know about it, or because you do it so instinctively, you've forgotten that it's a learned skill at all?

Here's how it works:

- First, you are in a state of *unconscious incompetence*. That is, you don't know that you don't know how to do something. For example, if you have to learn to delegate in a new role, a skill you've never needed before, how would you even know that there's a tried and tested way of doing it? So you muddle along, giving instructions more or less as you've always done, and find yourself wondering why it isn't working…

- Then you enter into a state of *conscious incompetence*. That is, you become starkly aware your skills are lacking and you try and find ways to overcome the situation. Now at least you know what it is that you didn't know before. You can look it up, read about it, or go and get help.

>>>

- At some point, after a period of trial and error, you find out what you need to know and move into a state of *conscious competence*. You start to use the skill, becoming gradually less concerned with the mechanics of what you're doing. Remember when you first learned to drive? You probably remember over-thinking every move, maybe even muttering to yourself, 'mirror, signal, manoeuvre'… until one day you drive to work thinking about the day ahead, and realise that you've driven perfectly safely and competently without, by and large, having had to think about it at all. You've entered the state of…

- *Unconscious competence*: you use the skill so easily and naturally that you forget you ever couldn't do it. If others ask questions about it, you'll say things like, 'It's just common sense, really', and 'There's nothing to it'.

It would be a mistake, however, in your development as a leader just to stop there. OK, it's really good to have a natural ease about the things you have to do in your work, but unless you are willing to explore your own competence, you'll never be able to coach or develop, or even empathise with, someone who doesn't have your level of skill. Unpacking what you do so instinctively gives you, and therefore others, access to the same body of skills.

That's what this book does. It unpacks those skills which, when naturally and easily displayed, look so normal and effortless that it's easy to forget that real effort goes into learning and practising them. None of the skills we talk about in this book comes instinctively to human beings; they may *look* like normal everyday social skills, but there's a whole lot more to them than that. Remember that, and you'll find the process of exploring and practising these leadership skills more interesting – and tougher – than you might have expected.

The reward is one day to find that you've negotiated a tricky meeting, a confrontation with a colleague or a challenging sales presentation, and not only produced a successful, win–win outcome, but done it easily, gracefully and with unconscious competence. And, if you are willing to do the work of analysing and exploring how you produced the result you did, you can pass on your skills and methods to others, leaving your organisation the richer for it.

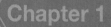

Chapter 1

Your organisation isn't 'yours', and your problems aren't all about 'them'

Working communication skill no. 1:
setting groundrules and holding effective
meetings

Chapter 1 – Your organisation isn't 'yours', and your problems aren't all about 'them'

- 'Why does everything end up on my desk?'
- 'Nobody shows any initiative – it's like managing a bunch of children.'
- 'Why can't I get people to do what I want them to do?'
- 'Unless I watch them like a hawk, they can't be trusted to behave in accordance with our values.'
- 'I do everything I can to look after them, yet they still complain about me behind my back.'

Are these, or something like these, familiar thoughts that keep you awake at night? Do you worry that people don't understand you and your well-meaning efforts on their behalf? Do you feel frustrated and angry that you can't seem to get them to do what you want and what your business needs? How much would it transform your working life if these worries weren't dominating your thoughts?

How much do you understand about how your organisation works? Not its finances, its published structure or its production cycle (which for the purposes of this book I am assuming you know and understand well), but the people issues, the culture, the mindsets and attitudes that cause your organisation either to be a great one, or one in which conflict, politics, fear and finger pointing thrive? It's an area of organisational life that like many leaders, you may regard as a bit of a mystery, a black art – one which gets solved only by luck (you recruit the right people) or effort (you troubleshoot constantly).

It's not a black art though. In my working life, these are common patterns: I see them every time I talk to business leaders, and the solutions are straightforward and easily learned. Once you know this, it's simply a matter of putting in a little effort to learn some new mindsets and a comprehensive set of key skills: those of *working* communication. The first thing to do is to explore your existing mindset, which just might be getting in your way…

The prevailing mindset

Cameron, a life-long property specialist, is the leader of a large division of a household-name property company in the UK. They are the market leader in their field and the business is doing very well, so it's clear that the employees are technically good at the 'property' side of their jobs, can mostly successfully create relationships with clients and sell property, usually better than the competition.

Internally, however, they have occasional problems with people and their behaviour, which show up in complaints, dissatisfaction and demotivation among colleagues and more junior employees – a warning sign that the internal culture of leadership and management is probably not as well managed as external relationships between the company and its market.

In discussions with Cameron about the business and how he would like to grow and develop the culture and the people, the conversation always goes something like this: 'We have a problem with Alex – he rubs people up the wrong way and his team is complaining about him. Is there anything you can do to help us turn him into the leader we'd like him to be?' ... 'And then there's Nadia. She just never quite delivers what she promises. She sounds willing when you ask her to do something, but then somehow doesn't deliver on time, or sometimes at all. Can you give her a few sessions of coaching so she improves?'

In other words, it usually feels as if we are being asked to fix people problems, one at a time, on an ad hoc basis and very often rather too late in the day (the best time to sort out problems is to come in before they have gone wrong and people have become rattled and upset). It's difficult to convey to Cameron that there might be another way of doing things, or that he might consider bringing us in before relationships are at crisis point, because his current mindset only allows him to consider one type of solution.

Cameron views the source of people issues as residing in *individuals*. He focuses on a person's personality, skills and competence in managing themselves and relating to others, and draws a conclusion as to whether they are doing things right or wrong. He tends to view an individual, like Alex or Nadia, as the *source* of a problem and may even blame them for the trouble he feels they cause. This leads to solutions like mandatory coaching sessions or counselling to remedy their behaviour.

Alex or Nadia may indeed have issues and could well change their behaviour after coaching, counselling, being warned or being given feedback to raise their performance. But managing people this way is like playing one of those fairground games where you bash down one pop-up with a big hammer, only to have another, and then another and another pop up elsewhere. You never win.

This is typical of the way many leaders think about others in their working (and indeed often their personal) circle. Indeed, if it were possible to pick off people one at a time and fix them, life would be easy. However, life is rarely this simple: it is nearly always unfair to assume that the solution to a complex problem lies in one individual, and, people being what they are, it's almost never possible to fix them in any case. They tend to resent being blamed for an issue at work and regarded as a problem, and this can lead to their resisting the coaching, even when they might under other circumstances be receptive. It makes your job and ours very difficult.

This perspective also causes leaders great stress, because everything seems to come back to them and their ability to diagnose and fix the people in their organisation.

They feel much like dog walkers holding the leads of a number of separate dogs, each of which has a different training issue. They might be able to hold and manage three, four or even six leads, but two hundred? A thousand? Clearly, this mindset and the only solutions that it seems to permit become far too much to manage as an organisation grows.

There is a way of understanding how organisations work that demystifies what is going on and gives you a handle on how to tackle the issues that arise. Get your head around this mindset, and you will be able to manage and develop your organisation so it starts to run smoothly by itself, and individuals will not only need less of your direct hands-on input, but will actively start to regulate themselves and lighten your load. You will then be able to lead the organisation by standing back and applying little tweaks and adjustments as needed, where now you may well feel that if you were to let go of your iron control of the situation, everything would just fall apart – indeed you may have tried it, and proved to yourself that it won't work.

This is because the people you lead have been trained (by you) to believe this is the only way of doing things. If you suddenly release your hold, of course they will be surprised and fall into disarray – they too lack the mindset and the training they need to take over self-management from you. Read on for an alternative picture of how it could work...

A more productive mindset

There is a point, when human beings come together, that a group of individuals becomes an organisation in its own right. Like a hive of bees, the group becomes, however fleetingly, an *organism*. And organisms have rules of their own that, when they are operating at their best, override a narrow focus on individuals and their behaviour. Formal groupings of people take on a life of their own and can learn to communicate and organise themselves in a different way from the way they would if they regarded themselves simply as a group of random individuals. This means that if you learn to spot the rules by which your particular organism operates, and focus on adjusting these to deliver the kind of behaviour you are looking for, you will often be surprised by the speed and impact of change for the better.

Think about that beehive. If, for the moment, we regard the beekeeper as the leader, how does he manage the hive? It would be crazy for him to take an individual bee and carry out a check on its health and wellbeing, or examine its function and how it carries out its role, in isolation from its group. The bee's behaviour only has meaning in the context of the hive and of its bee counterparts. And, for that matter, so does the beekeeper's.

Yet how often do we do exactly the same thing in our human organisations, from families to businesses? We talk about the problem child, the disruptive team member, the departmental silo that doesn't deliver. If we could only fix them and their behaviour, everything would be hunky dory – or so we think. In my work, this is very often the starting point for a conversation with a frustrated business leader, and he or she nearly always asks me to help resolve the problem from the perspective of the *individual*.

Many leaders miss this essential insight. We are so conditioned in Western society to focus on the individual – his or her rights, duties, character, personality, skills, attributes and faults – that we tend to manage our lives and work from this standpoint. It's part of the essential survival mechanism of a human being to focus from a very early age essentially on our own needs ahead of those of others – observe any toddler! So, though we become socialised as we grow into adulthood, most people retain this primary focus. When push comes to shove, we look after ourselves and our own, ahead of the group, team, community or organisation. Thinking in terms of a team, a group or an organisation has to be *learned*.

People in groups behave in the way they do *because* they work with others – they are all part of one organism, like the bees in a hive. You, as its leader, are part of the organism too; you're a reflection of it and it of you. It's impossible to fix any one individual, or yourself, without causing a knock-on effect elsewhere in the hive.

So it's not about you *or* them. It's not you *versus* other people, though I know it sometimes feels that way. The company, the team, the group isn't yours – even if in legal terms you happen to own it. It has a life of its own, and comprises not just you, but many other people too – employees, interns, customers, suppliers, contractors – who interact with each other and influence the group's behaviour.

The vast majority of people don't come to work to do a bad job and be disruptive. The individual you are worried about doesn't want to be a problem – and it's almost always not an individual problem anyway. They are only like that in the hive of their team, family or organisation (family therapists have cottoned on to this, and always work with the whole family in the room). So the answer isn't to take an individual person or even an individual department and fix them in isolation. Lead and manage the hive as a whole: examine its environment, its interactions, the written and unwritten rules it operates by and the focus (individual or group) of its members. And *don't do it by yourself* – that's just more of the same.

How would it be if you got together with the whole group and worked *together* to resolve any issues you had with others and their behaviour? Maybe Nadia would stop missing deadlines and making promises she won't fulfil if her whole working group created an agreement that they all wouldn't do that in the future. Maybe Alex would stop rubbing people up the wrong way if those people let him know to his face, kindly and unemotionally, that his behaviour upsets them, instead of gossiping and complaining behind his back. And maybe if each individual member of the group looked to his or her *own* behaviour, without pointing fingers, the whole group would work more effectively together.

Everything is a team issue

With this new mindset, you will regard the group, team or small organisation as a system, made up of the sum of the parts, but with its own set of behaviours and patterns that go beyond those of the individual members. You can't explain away people's behaviour only by reference to their personality or style, because you cannot discount the influence of the group mentality. Groups have a strong effect on group members and arouse powerful feelings, of excitement, warmth and inclusion, and of anxiety, concern (what is my status? do I belong?) and discomfort. Your job as a leader is to help the group encourage and harness the positive feelings, and minimise and control the negative.

People use different behaviours and strategies to cope in groups, and therefore you must deal with these behaviours and strategies *in the group* – they have no meaning outside it. How often have you met someone who is cooperative, sociable and friendly in their private life, and moody, resistant and abrasive at work – or the other way around? Perhaps you are aware that you show up as a different person in the different groups you belong to? That's because, without being consciously aware of it, you allow the group to influence the way you behave.

There is no point trying to deal with each person at the level of the individual, whether you are dealing with a family, a work group or a sports team – all the players in a situation are equally responsible (not to blame) for the dynamics that arise. Even two individuals create their interaction patterns *together* (think of the different patterns that arise between cohabiting couples), and, if part of a larger group, create their behaviour and coping strategies as part of the group. Taking this perspective, you may tend to focus more on raising each individual's awareness of their style and of their impact on others. You might want also to examine yourself in the same way – in fact I'd recommend you do.

Once you have acknowledged that you are an intrinsic part of the group dynamic, it will very quickly become obvious that you cannot do this work on yourself except by observing yourself as *part* of the group. This is why much of my work involves facilitating and coaching groups to see their own patterns and helping them to negotiate more constructive ones – you need an uninvolved outsider to hold up a mirror to you collectively so that you can see and explore your own patterns. It's also why, in working with groups, I always insist on having the whole group, with its leader, and nobody else, in the room.

What we call *culture* at work is the sum total of the assumptions, rules, beliefs and attitudes by which we operate. We pick these up from the people around us. We train new recruits in them within the first few weeks of their appointment. And we learn to operate inside the restraints they place on us, almost without realising it. Culture usually just *evolves*. In the absence of a conscious focus on creating the groundrules by which people should regulate their behaviour, they will just make them up on the basis of observation, gossip and hearsay. People learn things like, 'It's not OK to admit to mistakes around here', 'You can't leave the building until the boss goes home' and 'It's OK to turn up late to things, because everyone else does'. Before you know where you are, your organisation is being regulated by a host of unwritten, and unexamined, rules and assumptions that would probably horrify you.

I DON'T THINK SMITHERS UNDERSTANDS OUR COMPANY CULTURE

As your organisation grows, small group issues become wider organisational issues. For example, if part of your organisation is going through downsizing, those people may feel threatened. They in turn will talk to others and this may give rise to a pattern of defensive behaviour elsewhere in the organisation, often lasting years beyond the originating series of events. If you are very warm-hearted and inclusive as a leader, tending to let people off if they make mistakes or underperform, then this pattern will very quickly spread through your organisation. Or if managers feel they experience threatening or bullying behaviour from the top, they may pass on this management style to their teams, even though it's not their natural preference.

These unexamined patterns form your organisational culture and, unless you're very lucky, it's rare for it to develop naturally in the direction of cooperation, inclusivity and partnership – human beings don't always work that way, and there are too many dysfunctional beliefs out there about business and organisational life for your culture to grow by chance in that direction. That's the problem with most business cultures – they aren't *designed* to support the organisation, they're just left to happen, so quite often the culture that evolves ends up at odds with the strategic direction of the company.

One client company, a big global name in freight transport and logistics, had been through a major turnaround, during which they reassessed much about the business, completely altering their pricing structure and rationalising their client base. They had been in trouble, needing emergency measures and a lot of hard work to survive. An entirely appropriate culture of long hours and crisis management emerged during this period.

By the time I was invited by a talented and dynamic senior director, Angelo, to work with his senior team, the business had enjoyed three or four years of consolidation and profitable trading. The strategy had been to use the newly consolidated base of streamlined processes to go for growth and it was paying off.

But the culture hadn't caught up. The senior team were trapped in a loop of firefighting, quick-fix problem-solving, long hours and diving into the minutiae. Other people were increasingly frustrated that there was no direction from above, and no role for them while management had its hands on every detail. Good people started to leave and employee surveys showed morale to be very low. Angelo, as a relatively new leader from outside the company, wanted to challenge this pattern.

To Angelo, with his experience in other organisations, it was obvious that no one had stopped to examine the organisation culture inherited from the old era and question its appropriateness for the new era. After undertaking a systematic process of exposing and questioning the old era culture, and designing and embedding a new set of mindsets and practices for the business's new direction, the slow drain of dissatisfied people was reversed and results started to improve markedly.

This is why the pressure on leaders to 'walk the talk' is so critical – your behaviour sets a standard that is copied throughout the organisation. That's why this book takes *you* and *your* behaviour as the starting point for change. A crucial part of your role as an organisational leader is to set the direction for the culture you'd like your organisation to have, to role model it, and to install the platforms (management structures, meetings, processes etc.) and the training to ensure that people's behaviour and performance reflect the organisational culture you are designing. Organisational culture needs to be consciously *designed* and *managed*: generally speaking, good ones don't just evolve.

When you really understand this, your role and that of other leaders in your group or company can change. You no longer have to control from the front, dragging the organisation along by extraordinary effort and the force of your personality. Recognising that your organisation has its own dynamics, you become more of a custodian. Your job is to set the direction for, and to *take care* of, this growing entity, not to control it. Like a beekeeper, you need to manage the hive's environment and the resources it needs to survive and to thrive, not maintain a laser focus on every individual bee. If you've read this far, you already know that won't be possible as your organisation grows. Even if it were possible – say, if your organisation were very small – it's exhausting, and you have better things to do.

This mindset will free you up to do the right things to grow your business, to achieve inspiring targets, and to empower people and grow them into future leaders.

Some vital conversations to have with others in your organisation

These are all conversations that you and your colleagues should hold *together* – with outside help if you find it at all difficult. Don't sit behind a closed door and produce the answers yourself – that's falling into the very trap you are trying to avoid. *Negotiate* the rules and thrash out solutions that work for everybody. That way everybody takes ownership of the groundrules and the behaviour, and you as leader no longer need to pull the strings personally with each individual or department.

- Where are we going and are we all really on board?
- What are our values?
- What behaviour is and isn't acceptable between us?
- To what extent does each of us role model our values and behaviours *without exception*?
- What are the basic groundrules around here, and what should they be?
- How should we run our meetings?
- Who is accountable for what and to whom?
- What does it actually mean to be accountable anyway?

How do you apply this mindset to your leadership?

- Catch, and stop, yourself explaining problems by complaining about individuals and devising ways of fixing them.
- Develop your ability to resolve what may be happening by focusing on the team or group in which the individuals are operating.
- When a team is troubled, ask what's going on in the team.
- Encourage the team to take responsibility as a whole. If individual members are unhappy, not performing or behaving dysfunctionally, it's a team issue.
- Let others find their own solutions, as long as they are good enough. Don't disempower people by insisting they do everything exactly the way you would do it.
- Hire an external facilitator who specialises in teams to allow you to participate in this work as a member of your team, not an outsider.
- Examine yourself, what you are feeling and what role you might play in generating the kind of behaviour you would rather not happen.
- As your organisation grows, take responsibility yourself and encourage others to take more responsibility for what is happening in your organisation.

Working communication skill no. 1:
setting groundrules and holding
effective meetings

Any committee that is the slightest use is composed of people who are too busy to want to sit on it for a second longer than they have to.

Katharine Whitehorn

In far too many organisations, I see meetings where people arrive late and unprepared. Sometimes participants openly check their emails, or even answer their phone and leave the room for a while to take a call. Even where gadgets are switched off, people are frequently not listening to each other. They talk over each other, interrupt or start side conversations while someone is speaking.

... AND NOW I'D LIKE TO TURN TO SLIDE 254A

Practices like these damage relationships and hinder productivity. They betray the presence of unconscious attitudes and beliefs such as:

• 'I don't see the point of this meeting.'
• 'I've got far too much to do to be here.'

>>>

Working communication skill no. 1:
setting groundrules and holding
effective meetings

- 'My attention is not needed for this bit/this bit is boring – I'll tune back in when we are talking about something more interesting (to me).'
- 'I feel threatened; I have to defend myself/my function/my profession at all costs.'

Sometimes meetings have no clear agenda, or only a simple list of topics to be discussed with no indication of the intended outcome. And all too often people leave with no idea of what exactly is to be done, and by whom. So nothing happens, and all that time and effort comes to nothing.

What's the alternative?

How would it be instead if:

- Every person in the meeting knows exactly why they are there and what their contribution is expected to be.
- Only the right people are there.
- Everybody turns up in good time, fully prepared.
- Everyone switches off their phone for the duration of the meeting.
- All listen fully and without interrupting to each person speaking.
- People tell the truth without fear of reprisals.
- You can trust others to keep their word.
- There is a clear agenda, with clear objectives for each item.
- Actions with a deadline date are assigned to named individuals for every decision made.
- The meeting finishes on time.

Many organisations start their cultural revolution by working hard at transforming the quality and quantity of outcomes from their meetings. To have constructive meeting practices become 'just the way we do things round here', you need to do some conscious design work. Some of the most important work you ever do is done in meetings – so spend some time making sure that they are as effective and efficient as possible.

>>>

1. Consider what you would like the meeting to achieve – its SMART objectives (specific, measurable, agreed, realistic, time bound; see p50) – *in specific measurable terms*:

   - A decision on…
   - A plan to achieve…
   - A list of…
   - Clear objectives for…
   - The go-ahead to…

2. In the light of the goals, consider carefully who needs to be at the meeting – *and who doesn't*.

3. Issue an agenda, stating each item as a SMART objective, and assigning a realistic time to it. Most people try to achieve far too much in one meeting. Three to five items will be more than enough for a two-hour meeting.

4. Assign time at the beginning of the meeting to issue and draw attention to the groundrules, and at the end of the meeting to review briefly how it went and set up the next meeting.

5. If you include 'Any other business' at the end of the agenda, allow no more than five minutes for it and enforce this rigorously. Any topic that fails to be handled within this time should be given its own (timed) slot on the next meeting's agenda.

6. Issue a basic set of groundrules and at the first meeting where you use these, assign an agenda slot (timed) to discuss and complete the list. At the very least you should have groundrules for:

   - Attendance and timekeeping
   - Mobile technology usage
   - Listening and participation
   - Accountability for actions
   - Confidentiality
   - Decision making

7. State each groundrule in clear behavioural terms: not for example, 'Be respectful', but 'Make your points concisely', 'Hear people out without interrupting', 'Arrive on time and well-prepared'.

>>>

Working communication skill no. 1:
setting groundrules and holding
effective meetings

8. Always explicitly remind people of the groundrules at the beginning of meetings and review their use at the end. After a while, participants will get used to applying them almost unconsciously.

9. There is no need for most business meetings to keep narrative minutes at all. Simply record actions as a list with three columns headed 'Action', 'Who accountable' and 'By/on/from when'. Train yourself and others to sum up each agenda item in the form of a clear, measurable action, and record this on the list before moving on. Agree the wording carefully with the members of the meeting and don't move on until you are sure that the action is clear and unambiguous and that someone has taken full accountability for it.

10. If a report or policy or any other lengthier document needs to be drawn up following the discussion, assign an action in the action list for the accountable person to write it up and produce a draft for all to review (don't record detailed content in the action list – that's the accountable person's job). Put a slot – timed – to hold this review on the agenda for a future meeting.

11. Always include specific target dates in the action list: if you create it as an Excel spreadsheet, you can sort the items by the date column. As items are completed, clear the date, but keep the item. When you sort by date, these items will end up at the top or bottom of the list, but you will still be able to refer to them if you want to remind yourself what was done and by whom. Review and update the action list at every meeting.

Chapter 2

'Everybody wants promotion, but someone's got to do the work'

Working communication skill no. 2:
working *on* your business

Chapter 2 – 'Everybody wants promotion, but someone's got to do the work'

- 'They all want a pay rise – but we're not making enough money.'
- 'Nobody documents anything – we fly by the seat of our pants.'
- 'I never know what's going on until it's an emergency.'
- 'All I seem to do is make myself unpopular.'

Do you sometimes feel like this? There comes a point in an organisation's early growth when communication seems to break down. It's no longer small and informal enough for everyone to know what's going on by listening in on conversations, yet it is not a corporate entity either, with layers of process and structures, resources and staff to help the operation run smoothly.

You feel out of control and can't keep your arms round everything that's going on. People seem to expect things like pay rises, bonuses, development and promotion, but complain if you ask them to document their work or be accountable for measurable results. You're frustrated and people are starting to complain. What's happening? Your organisation has grown up – it's now a second generation company.

The prevailing mindset

Lisa is the MD of her family's well regarded and growing marketing services company. She has worked hard over the past couple of years to move away from the all-hands-to-the-pump, slightly chaotic start-up phase of the company in the hands of her brilliant and very entrepreneurial father, John. With the aid of her brother and co-director Ian, she's putting in structures and processes to systematise the running of the company. She also has one eye to the future – she knows that if she and her family one day want to sell the business, prospective buyers will expect it to be run in a stable and professional manner, without the vulnerability of being dependent on any one individual with all the vital knowledge in his or her head.

However, some people liked the cosy, informal family feel of the company before Lisa took over, and they are uncomfortable with her emphasis on accountability, management structure and results. They complain that they aren't getting enough money and one or two of the younger team members have an eye on promotion. Yet they still resist the changes, which they feel are too 'corporate', preferring to do things in the old, slightly haphazard way that meant nobody felt too on the spot when things went wrong. Lisa feels unsupported, and as if she can do nothing right.

A two-part model of organisations

Lisa's employees have two basic perceptions of an organisation – on the one hand, there's the cosy, family-style, slightly chaotic, first generation (1G) start-up where everyone feels vital to the business and, when things are going well, a sense of achievement and belonging. On the other, there's the big corporate, in which (in their perception) an individual is just a cog in a machine, and fun, innovation and self-expression are stifled. Lisa's is a marketing services company in an industry in which most of the players fit the former picture, and it's this chaotic but fun and creative image that has attracted them to work in Lisa's family business.

Many people's picture of any organisation larger than a start-up is based on years of being in school and maybe college, and of reading about big third generation (3G) companies in the news, where the headline stories tend to be about bonuses (especially in recent years), promotion and huge salaries.

This simple and very common model of organisations leads to assumptions about the way organisations work, which give rise to the problems Lisa and her employees are struggling with:

- 'After a year or so I'll get a salary increase (they always seem to in the stories I read in the papers).'
- 'After a short time in my first job, I'll get promotion (I got one every year at school).'
- 'My job is my opportunity to express myself and learn the things I need for my CV.'
- 'My boss is there to a) tell me what to do and b) look after me.'
- 'I'll get on if I make lots of effort and get on well with my colleagues.'

A different kind of organisation

But in the middle, between the 1G start-ups and the 3G corporations, there's a third possible type of business – the second generation (I'll call them 2G) organisations. These are small to medium-sized enterprises (SMEs), and in the UK at least, account for more than 90 per cent of all businesses and employ over 12 million people. It's a very wide definition: if your business is an SME, according to the European Union (EU) definition, it will be turning over anything from £2m to £50m and employ from 10 to 250 people.

EU definition of an SME:

- Micro business = less than 10 employees and turnover under €2 million.
- Small business = less than 50 employees and turnover under €10 million.
- Medium business = less than 250 employees and turnover under €50 million.

See: European Commission. (2015) 'What is a SME?' Online at: http://ec.europa.eu/growth/smes/business-friendly-environment/sme-definition/index_en.htm

Even some well-known household names – one very well known global property ser-vices company for example – have many of the characteristics of an SME, because of their values and the way they are structured into smaller units.

2G organisations need to be structured more than start-ups, but this doesn't mean corporate structures – in fact people moving to them from corporates very often fail precisely *because* they over-structure and over-engineer the organisation. It's this 2G type of company towards which Lisa and Ian are working, and they will probably never choose to grow beyond it.

If you are one of the many business leaders who resist structure because you as-sociate it with being corporate – maybe you even left corporate life to get away from what you perceived as too much structure and control – you may be in danger of throwing the baby out with the bathwater. And if you are an employee who came to a smaller organisation because you thought it would be all about informality and fun and nothing else, then you'll need to think again.

A more productive mindset

The 2G company doesn't need the full raft of corporate struc-tures to work well – for example it won't usually have full-time internal service departments like HR, finance, marketing or IT, instead using the services of part-timers, agencies and external suppliers. This will come as good news to Lisa's employees, who fear the rigid-ity of a corporate environment. But it will still need *some* basic structures and rules to make it work, and it helps a great deal if everybody understands and accepts this.

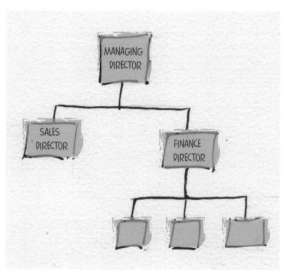

How do I know my organisation is moving on?

Take a look at Table 1 on p37.

When a 1G organisation is working...

If a 1G organisation still has plenty of life in it, you should expect your main experience to be one of excitement, fun and achievement. It's a roller-coaster ride of juggling new business opportunities and doing the work needed to fulfil orders on a just in time basis – sometimes *only* just in time! Your main business focus will be on cash flow – on getting the business, getting paid and keeping costs as low as possible. This will often mean a few people doing all the work, and at its best, the sense of teamwork and cooperation will be amazing. You won't have enough people, nor many systems, if any at all, and a lot of 'how we do things around here' will exist in people's heads, partly because you are working it out as you go along. As a leader, you should expect to be very hands-on and there will be nobody to delegate to, so you'll need to get your sleeves rolled up. Your main issues in developing this young organisation will be keeping everybody motivated and making sure all of you maintain some sort of work–life balance.

When it's time to move on...

When the buzz of the initial period has worn off, you'll start to notice signs that the organisation needs to move into the next phase. The first thing you'll probably notice is that it doesn't feel like fun any more, and the juggling, instead of being a challenge, is just frustrating. Employees are starting to complain and point fingers and may even start to leave. A build-up of mistakes and poor service may threaten good relations, and you may start to lose customers.

What to work on in the early 2G stage

Now's the time to start to get to grips with the chaos by putting in simple structures and processes to make sure that things don't get missed. You don't need expensive computer systems, but some basic checklists and manuals will ensure that you capture what works so you no longer have to depend on just one person to get it right. You'll be growing by now, and other people will take over some of the work, so it's even more important to document your basic processes. As more people join your organisation, it will start to be possible for individuals to specialise so that there isn't so much duplication or treading on toes. They can get training too, so that the whole operation begins to become more professional.

One of the challenges for you as a leader at this stage will be learning to let go and trust others to do the work. As your organisation grows, you will not be able to continue to do everything yourself, and your role will become one of training, coaching, developing and supporting people – but *not* doing their jobs. In the early 2G phase, you and your co-directors should start to think longer term. Where are you taking the business? What do you want to achieve in two years', four years' and ten years' time?

HE LIKES TO KEEP A TIGHT REIN ON HIS STAFF

And what do you want your business to stand for? While you had your hands all over it in the early stages, it was relatively easy to make sure that the business delivered the quality you wanted, the promises you made to your market were kept and your customers got the service you believed they should. But now other people are working on those things for you. Now you need to *articulate* these values, beliefs and principles so that your larger and growing organisation continues to be a true representation of them. You need to stop working *in* your business and start working *on* it.

When it's time to move on

Your organisation may stay in the 2G stage for much of its life. As I've already said, many business leaders and owners enjoy working in this kind of organisation and have chosen to do so – they will not want to grow much beyond a couple of hundred people at most. They certainly won't want the complex corporate governance involved in becoming a 3G organisation. Having said that, towards the later stages of your organisation's 2G existence, you'll start to see the signs that the organisation is straining to move on again.

Life has become comfortable, without too many scares and surprises, but perhaps you and your co-directors have an uneasy feeling that people still depend on you too much, and you cannot see any future leaders stepping up to knock at your doors. On the other hand, people are starting to complain that they are feeling unchallenged and you'll see finger pointing between different parts of the organisation. It always amazes me how this can happen even in very small organisations – sales will have a dig at marketing, and production has its complaints about the designers – when each department is only two or three people and sits just around the corner. Time to give them all more accountability…

What to work on in the late 2G stage

A good rule of thumb at this stage of your organisation's development is to ask yourself, even if you have no intention of selling, what a future potential purchaser of your company would look for. Certainly they will want a healthy order book, a solid reputation and stable finances, but more than that, they will look for evidence of a strong management group, without heavy dependence on a few key players, and motivated people who are well trained and know their jobs, with a positive can-do culture. That way, a possible purchaser knows the company won't fall apart because one key player leaves, or all the employees take the opportunity to jump ship because they're so dissatisfied.

Now is the time consciously to pass accountability down from the director group to your key senior managers. If no future leaders immediately spring to mind, then all your efforts now should be targeted at bringing on, or finding, the right people. You may need to ask yourself some tough questions: why has nobody shown up so far? And why are you still doing so much troubleshooting and micro-managing? Could *you* be the reason why you don't seem to attract go-getters who step eagerly up to take responsibility for the business? You might need to examine just how committed you and your co-directors are to letting go and passing accountability down the line: this means exposing and working on your own mindsets about your role in the business. Many senior business leaders who do this work realise that they really do not want to let go at all, and they may have to make uncomfortable decisions about their future and that of their business as a result.

One of the symptoms of this resistance is doing a lot of structural re-engineering on the business – recruiting, pay rises, bonuses etc. – in an attempt to attract and motivate the right kind of people, instead of focusing on changing your and everybody else's mindset. It's a warning sign that you and your co-directors would prefer the solution to lie in the relatively easy arena of throwing money at the problem, rather than doing the hard and sometimes uncomfortable work of changing your mindsets and your behaviour. You cannot lead and manage the business at this stage with the mindsets and behaviours from a previous stage.

- Start to work *on* the business, as well as *in* it. It's a difficult balance to strike, but your job as leader of the organisation is to step outside it from time to time and look at how it's shaping up. What does it need? How can you fill the gaps that emerge as it grows? You can't do this if you're just one of the bees.
- Make yourself step back and let others do the work. I've met business leaders who empty the bins because 'nobody else seems to notice it's needed'. Well, they never will if you go on doing it. Your job is to motivate someone else to empty the bins, while you get on with designing the future shape of your organisation.
- Think hard about what you want in the future (with your co-directors if relevant). Then paint a picture in inspiring language, and keep painting it, every time you talk to the people working in your organisation. Don't frame it and hang it on the wall – *talk* endlessly about your vision, your standards, your values, your customers. Infect people with your enthusiasm for the enterprise you are in together.
- Keep developing systems and processes as the business grows – but don't get seduced by the big all-singing, all-dancing packages that the big 3G companies use. They'll be over-engineered for your needs. Keep it as simple as possible at every stage.

The Entrepreneurial Model has less to do with what's done in a business and more to do with how it's done. The commodity isn't what's important – the way it's delivered is.

Michael E. Gerber

The idea of working *on* as opposed to *in* your business is an easy concept to grasp, but after some years of working in your business as one of the team, fixing, troubleshooting and juggling along with everyone else, not as easy to learn to apply it consistently in practice.

WE NEED TO REMAIN FOCUSED ON OUR PRIORITIES AND NOT GET DISTRACTED BY EVERY SHINY NEW... OOH, LOOK – SQUIRREL!"

Working *in* your organisation is working on all those concrete, visible and tangible things that have got you through the start-up phase of your operation. By now you and your team are pretty good (or should be) at administration, organisation, cash flow, production, order fulfilment and so on.

>>>

To work on your organisation, you'll need to train yourself to spot things which at first will not seem as concrete, visible and tangible as you are used to. You'll also need to develop a new set of skills with which to work on them. Here are some questions to get you started:

- How motivated do people seem?
- Is there a dysfunctional level of gossip and finger pointing?
- Do you see practices and behaviour in your team that make you uncomfortable?
- Do you despair of getting others to abide by your values and standards?
- Are you and your fellow directors spending most of your time working in the business, or micro-managing others?
- Does it feel like everything's about the day to day and you've lost sight of where you are going?
- Are you and others in the business always running to keep up with the work-load, never on the front foot?
- Do you wonder about who will be capable of leading the business when you leave it?

As leader of your organisation, your sense of ownership will be huge, and it's much harder actually to stop doing things yourself than you might at first think. Now you need to learn to talk to people in a way that will motivate them to buy in to your vision for the business, your values and your standards. Many leaders assume at this point that people will just naturally copy how you do things, but adult human beings just don't work like that. They need to understand and buy in to the reasons for doing things in a certain way – and you need to learn how to help them do it.

Tell them what you are trying to achieve, not how *you* would do it

One of the first things to tackle is to articulate your standards in a way that allows others to apply them in their work, not by following slavishly each step you would take, but by understanding the essence of what it is you are saying, and finding their own way, in their own style, of achieving the same outcome. This will need some careful thought, and is best achieved by always considering the outcome you want to achieve, not the exact steps you personally would take to achieve it.

Designing a checklist and training everyone to follow it is a lot of work for you and incredibly demotivating and boring for them. They won't sound enthusiastic and natural if they're trying to follow a script.

Take the example of customer service when it's done by an organisation that has tried to achieve conformity by doing it this way. It seems that certain organisations teach their staff to call total strangers, address them by their first name, and as the opening gambit for a sales conversation ask, 'And how are you today?' Do you ever use this as your opening question when you've called a person you've never spoken to before? Of course you don't – the natural way to start this conversation is to introduce yourself very briefly and say why you've called. But somebody wrote this script, and now hundreds of call centre staff follow it slavishly and sound like robots.

If asked, members of your team may have an even better, and certainly more personal, idea for engaging someone's interest and connecting with them – that's why there's no point your trying to train them in your or anyone else's way of doing it. Instead, tell them what you are trying to achieve, and start a conversation with them about this outcome, how they see it and how *they personally* would take steps to achieve it.

In the conversation, you'll be able to hear if any of them have ideas that don't fit your picture and you'll be able to explain and clarify it again. Your team will almost certainly have good ideas of their own, and if you are willing to listen, you will together come up with a composite way of achieving the original outcome that is even better than the method you came up with by yourself.

More importantly, you'll have transferred your original vision to your team, and they will all now be bought in to achieving the same standard of service. They will feel empowered to express this aspect of the organisation's values in their own way and you won't need to watch them like a hawk.

>>>

Watch for the warning signs

Take a look at Table 1 – this makes clear what is happening at each stage of your organisation's growth, what the warning signs are, and what there is to work on.

Table 1 – Stages of your organisation's growth

Level of organisation	What is happening in the company?	What to work on	How will you know it's time to make changes?
1G – start-up	• Entrepreneurial leadership • Few employees – up to 8 or 9 • Control from the centre • All hands to the pump • High-energy, fun • Juggling, troubleshooting • Adrenaline high, buzz • Focus on cash flow above all else	• Work–life balance • Working on as well as in the business • Communication • Working together effectively • Keeping people motivated • Recognition • Time management • Financial awareness • Cash flow	• Working harder just to stand still • People leaving • Trusted people demotivated • Differences over direction among leaders • Frustration and finger pointing • Losing customers • Rapid changes in policy • Repeated mistakes • Waste – processes, money, time

>>>

Level of organisation	What is happening in the company?	What to work on	How will you know it's time to make changes?
2G – consolidation	• 10 to 100+ employees • The organisation has developed a life of its own – hard to keep tabs on everything • Still directly led by the director(s): business development, troubleshooting, resolving conflict • Beginnings of second tier of management/ leaders • Focus on consolidation, building durable processes and systems	• Vision, values, strategy • Team develop-ment – communi-cation, role clarity, accountability, partnership • Delegation from leaders to managers at the next level • Creating a solid second tier of management • Motivation • Performance and behaviour standards – best practice • Leadership and management skills • Emergence of future leaders • Consistent, durable manage-ment systems and structures • Platforms for the culture to be discussed and reviewed	• Overdependence on directors • No future leaders coming through • Silos developing • Finger pointing and blame vs accountability • Narrow focus on one or two areas of the business balanced scorecard • Performance management stale and formulaic • Inability to adapt/ innovate • Complaints about bureaucracy • Talk about 'the old days' • Structural re-engineering going on – recruiting, restructuring, pay awards, bonuses etc., instead of addressing and resolving problems head on

>>>

Level of organisation	What is happening in the company?	What to work on	How will you know it's time to make changes?
3G – structure and control	• Owned by shareholders • Controlled by board of directors on behalf of the shareholders • Authority to manage day-to-day operations vested in officers • Emphasis on rigorous business planning • Hierarchy, departmentalisation • Structured organisation • Rigorous measurement of performance to support the organisation's purpose • Director-led strategy and growth	• Vision and strategy: clarity of purpose • A balanced scorecard • Performance management • Succession planning • Developing top performers • Transferring full ownership and accountability for the development of the organisation to second-tier management and beyond • Delegation • Recognition • Unity of culture • Continuous improvement	• Poor performance • Need to address new trends or market changes • Flabbiness – unprofitable areas, costs out of control, too many levels • Organisation structure out of date/doesn't meet current needs • Poor corporate governance • No vision – going through the motions

Some hints

- Train yourself to stand back from your organisation and spot the warning signs when it starts to creak as it grows.

- Develop your skills to be able actively to confront organisational, in addition to conventional business, issues.

- The skills you've used up to this stage to start up and work *in* your business are very different from the skills you now need to consolidate and work *on* your organisation – and that's what the rest of this book is about.

Chapter 3

The knowledge – how a second generation company works

Working communication skill no. 3: setting SMART objectives

Chapter 3 – The knowledge – how a second generation company works

There are many ways in which these middle-sized companies differ from the chaos of the start-up on the one hand, and the structure and resources of the corporate on the other. The ones I find have most impact on the way people communicate and work together are those to do with roles, accountabilities and managing performance.

Roles in the 2G organisation

The first thing to get your head around in the 2G company, is that *your job is not your own*. A very common belief among employees is that their role is in some way *theirs*, to serve their own personal needs for job satisfaction or for career growth, and this reflects a belief among leaders that you should tailor your management style to the skills and personality of the person you are managing.

In a typical start-up company, this may actually be possible: jobs are often created around whoever you've got available (family members, friends, children of existing team members, friends of friends), and so tend to be shaped around an individual's personality, skills and preferences. The role grows and changes shape as the person grows and changes. An individual can make him- or herself absolutely essential to the business and gain a great sense of personal achievement from doing so.

However, as the business grows too, and its needs change, this can leave it vulnerable.

One small and rapidly growing manufacturing company, with only a few employees, hired a receptionist, Carmen. Exceptionally capable and bright, Carmen gradually took over more and more. As well as receiving guests to the building, answering the phones and taking messages, she took over packing and shipping products and samples, handling customer queries, maintaining stock records and managing the health and safety recording system for the company. When a few years later she left, the company was twice the size it had been, and a new receptionist, Nicole, was hired.

It very quickly became clear that Nicole, while good at traditional receptionist duties, couldn't handle the complexity of the role Carmen had created, which needed a level of management ability and multitasking that Nicole simply hadn't expected. The problem was, they really needed another Carmen – and where were they going to find one of those? The solution was to return the receptionist role to the straightforward shape typical of that role, and to redistribute the other functions back to more appropriate roles elsewhere in the now larger organisation.

So as an organisation grows, it's necessary to make sure that roles serve the needs of the *business*, not those of the individual job holders. Bees have got this right. Each bee fills a predefined role in the hive. You can't imagine any one bee complaining that they feel bored and a lack of stretch in their job, so would like to take over part of someone else's job. Or that they would like to be promoted and get a bigger bonus as soon as they've filled their role for any length of time.

It's crucial that roles in the 2G company are designed to interlock with other roles such that there are no gaps or overlaps, and that when someone leaves, the role can easily be filled by someone new. Each role description also needs to contain accountability for delivering work in a simple, agreed and relatively standardised way. This means that the company is no longer dependent on individuals and that the roles are not so personalised and unique that no one else can do them.

Stay with me here – this doesn't mean that there is no space for individuals to grow, develop and be rewarded in a 2G organisation – quite the opposite. It's just that the mechanism works in a slightly different way from what many people expect.

Accountabilities in the 2G organisation

The starting point for designing a role in this way is *not* to start with the way it's being done now, by the current job holder. This is likely to be a reflection of two things: first, the start-up stage of the business, with a lot of duplication and overlap with other roles, and second, the job holder's skills and preferences. This is precisely what makes it so difficult to replace people in 1G organisations.

The role needs to be defined in terms of what it delivers to the business – a list of outputs (accountabilities) rather than a list of activities. It's not a list of 'what you do' (though most job descriptions we see are just this); it's an overview of what you can be counted on to deliver – hence 'accountabilities' – and it's *measurable*.

Table 2 is an example, for a senior financial adviser in a wealth management company.

You can see that the role is defined at a relatively high level, with five key accountabilities (four to six is ideal) for the job holder, each with a short list of its key measurement criteria. The job holder can maintain an overview in their own mind and so ensure that they are moving ahead in each area, the important long-term ones as well as the urgent short-term ones.

These accountabilities and measurement criteria must be negotiated and agreed with the job holder's manager and others so as not to overlap with other roles, or leave gaps, and can only be changed by agreement.

Table 2 – Example role description for a senior financial adviser

Accountabilities	Success measures
Ongoing, well-managed, sustainable business	• Shareholder value • Recovery rates on fee income • Time charges: fee capacity • Stakeholder satisfaction • Budget achievement
Well-maintained base of long-term, loyal and appreciative clients	• Target client wins • Referrals/testimonials • Recovery rates on fee income • Client feedback • Longevity/retention rates • % assets under management
Efficient and continually improving systems/processes	• Team member satisfaction • Client satisfaction • Margin • Write-offs
Outstanding financial and investment advice	• Industry recognition (awards etc.) • Benchmark data • Referrals/testimonials • Compliance checks • Client feedback • Director satisfaction
Satisfied and effective team	• Team member feedback/satisfaction • Team and individual objectives met

Defining a role in this way gives the job holder the chance to put their own stamp on *how* they achieve the outputs. Provided they meet the agreed success criteria and targets and work within company values and performance standards, they can do the job any way they want to. It's very different from being given a two-page list of tasks and activities to work through – and much more satisfying.

Promotion in the 2G organisation

The other thing that's often a surprise to employees (and, sadly, sometimes managers too) in a 2G organisation is the way promotion works. Here again there are two prevailing mindsets:

- 'So and so is a brilliant salesperson, teacher, project manager, doctor – we should promote her to management.'
- 'I've been in this job for two years and all my peers have been promoted – it's my turn now.'

Neither of these is true, and can cause problems. Think of the brilliant classroom teacher, who, promoted to head, now languishes in an office, drowning in a sea of paperwork. Or the talented project manager, who can handle tricky issues on site and excels at troubleshooting and getting the project in on time, but who lacks the tact and managerial skill to handle the complex organisational and personal issues that arise in his team back in the office.

You could be an absolutely brilliant project manager and still not be right for a head of projects role – it's a different job altogether – or an inspirational classroom teacher and no good at politics and administration. And you could have served your time in any role for many years: this still doesn't mean you're automatically ready for a more senior role – in fact it doesn't even mean you're doing every part of your current role as fully as you might. Because of the unexamined assumption that the purpose of doing any job is to fit yourself for the next one up, the organisational world is full of senior managers who have moved up the structure as the organisation grew, often without really filling the box fully in any role they have held.

The only way to be sure that someone is ready for promotion is to do what you would do if recruiting to that role for the very first time. Draw up a clear specification for the role and another for a hypothetical person you feel would best fit the role. Then match the person you've got against both the role spec and the hypothetical person spec – and *only employ them if there's a really good match*. And be careful of wishful thinking – it's probably a good idea to get an objective outsider involved in the recruitment in case your natural wish to make the role fit a person you have in mind causes you to miss something.

The key principle to remember is always that roles must serve the needs of the *business* itself, not the needs of the individual job holders, however deserving.

Managing performance in the 2G organisation

This principle for defining roles gives you a way of managing people's performance that is motivating and rewarding. See Figure 1.

Figure 1 – How fully rounded organisations work

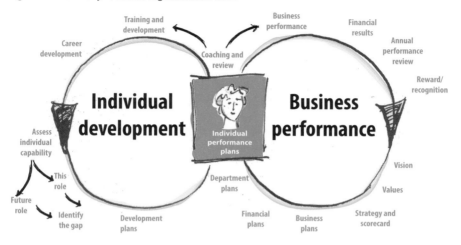

The organisation's performance

The right-hand circle is all about the business's performance. Your business may or may not have all the pieces in place, or at least not consciously (many successful businesses have very strong values and a vision in place though not consciously expressed). For our purposes though, this circle is about how the business's vision, values and strategy are connected to the work of each individual employee, and about how their work then comes together to deliver the overall results of the organisation.

It's this link that I see most often missing in my work with organisations. The idea of group targets and goals is often well established, at team, department and organisation level. But the final link in the chain, the link with the work of each individual in the organisation, is loosely drawn or even entirely missing. It's as if the leadership of the hive has communicated the message, 'make honey', but failed to identify clearly the role of each individual bee. You can see the result would be very similar to the 1G organisation – lots of well-meaning individuals running (flying!) around, getting in each other's way or duplicating effort. And it's not only very small organisations that make this mistake.

The crucial part of the diagram is the *individual performance plan*, which consists of two parts: a role description as described above, which identifies four to six accountabilities defined as key areas of *output*, together with the critical measurement criteria for each area, and a set of specific and measurable goals for each area of the role description.

This makes sure that every individual employee in the company, managers and senior leaders included, is doing exactly what the organisation needs him or her to do to achieve results in accordance with the company targets and values. As an organisation leader, you need to be very sure the right-hand circle is working well before even beginning to address the left-hand circle.

The individual's development

Many of the complaints of managers and employees come from an unexamined assumption that the left-hand circle is the whole purpose of their employment and indeed the organisation as a whole. People tend to think instinctively from an individual standpoint (what's in it for me?) and look for employment in organisations that will meet their personal needs. They need training and management to be encouraged to work in the interests of the whole.

But surely people work for reward?

The problem with reward is that we too often shortcut the whole issue, especially in the organisational world, by leaping to dishing out money, bonuses, promotions and benefits. This may not at first appear to be too much of a problem in an organisation that is awash with money (though the banking crisis gave us a graphic example of what can go wrong with this assumption) – but how many of those are there? Can you afford to give your employees premium salaries, large annual bonuses and cutting edge benefits? Probably not. And even if you could, I would argue that, in the long term, this is an unhealthy shortcut to take for the sake both of your employees and your organisation.

In the 2G organisation you will make problems for yourself if you allow each person to design their own job and goals to satisfy their personal preferences and development needs. Some people would certainly get job satisfaction if they were allowed to do this, but the effect on your organisation would be chaotic and very damaging. We've also said that your organisation probably cannot support using promotion as a way to motivate and reward people – it needs the right people in the right roles, doing exactly the right things, to make sure it runs efficiently.

So if you can't reward people by bending their job out of shape or by promoting them, how can you reward them? Well – *manage* them.

How do you apply this mindset to your leadership?
1. Focus on the right-hand circle and make sure that every individual has a role description like the one above, not just a list of activities to do.
2. Then ensure that, based on this role, they have a performance plan that is clearly connected to the organisation's vision, values and strategy.

3. Make sure each person has regular *and frequent* (at least monthly) one-to-one meetings with their manager, and support these meetings with every tool at your disposal: set them up for each of your own team members, never cancel them because the 'day job' gets in the way and never ask anyone else to cancel or postpone a one-to-one with one of their team to attend a meeting with you.

   At these meetings, which are *not* about work in progress or day-to-day troubleshooting, each employee has *one-to-one time with their own manager* during which they receive positive feedback on what they have achieved, and get the time, focus and help to achieve the things they find difficult. Even mature employees who don't need a lot of personal help will appreciate time with their manager to discuss the job and be acknowledged and recognised for their efforts.

4. Ensure that every individual job holder knows the degree to which they are achieving everything that's required of them in the role they hold; most people don't, because loose performance management means they are largely left to work out for themselves what is required of them, and they often haven't revisited their role description since the day they were employed. There is usually plenty of scope to give people additional challenging tasks, projects and targets without going outside their current role.

Pay people this amount of attention and you will find not only that your organisational results will improve, because everybody is now being held accountable for doing *all* of their job, but that individuals feel appreciated, motivated and, yes, rewarded. You only have to look at organisations operating in under-resourced areas, such as charity, the arts or alternative health, to see that it is possible for people to be incredibly motivated and satisfied for very little financial reward – *provided* they are managed, appreciated and acknowledged in this way.

When the right-hand circle is working tightly and well, and your organisation is delivering good financial and other results, then there will be the additional funds to give people salary increases and a bonus – not as a *substitute* for hands-on management, but as an added extra reward. There'll be extra resources for the training and development people crave. Your organisation will grow and there will be room to promote people who make the grade. The more the right-hand circle works, the more you can spin off into the left-hand circle.

And the more the left-hand circle works, the more successful your company will be, until you get a virtuous figure of eight working – all by making sure each bee in your hive knows what to do and gets the primary reward of knowing he or she is doing exactly what's required, and is fully acknowledged and appreciated for doing it.

Setting goals is the first step in turning the invisible into the visible.

Tony Robbins

Creating clear, measurable objectives and holding others to account for them is one of the most important practical skills of a leader. There is a real skill to capturing clearly and precisely the essence of what needs to be achieved, while making sure it is easily measurable – and that the measures and standards you use are the right ones.

A useful guide is to remember the acronym SMART. Your objectives should be: specific, measurable, agreed, realistic, time bound.

A SMART objective must be objectively measurable and/or observable – anybody should be able to see and agree that it has been achieved.

Easy objectives to set are those that address numerical targets:

- Achieve fee income of £xxx, by (date), with x per cent write-off rate.
- Make xxx prospect calls and set up xxx well-qualified meetings during (time period).
- Sign up xxx new clients in our target markets during (time period).
- Reduce costs by x per cent by (date).
- Develop and test client survey by (date). Administer to xx clients by (date). Report due by (date).
- Achieve client satisfaction of 75 per cent or above on client survey during (time period).
- Reduce the backlog of enquiries from xx to yy by (date).

Other objectives may address in-department projects, personal development needs and day-to-day behaviours. Agree measures with the job holder; you may need to be creative to ensure that the objective is *objectively* (i.e. by someone other than you) measurable and/or observable.

>>>

Use clear descriptive statements of the ideal outcome or behaviour you are aiming at:

- Improve accountability in my team this (time period).

  Measured by: improved quality of work (percentage right first time, number of trivial errors, etc.); supervision level reduced with no loss of quality (managerial time spent in hours/minutes); stakeholders are happy (director satisfaction, client satisfaction, etc.).

- Improve perception of self this year from one of resistance and lack of interest; accept feedback willingly.

  Measured by: unsolicited feedback (number of instances); formal review (manager and colleagues); 360 degree feedback.

- Improve meeting of deadlines in my team.

  Measured by: improved quality of work (percentage right first time, number of trivial errors etc.); deadlines missed (target = 0); time freed to focus on other tasks (time freed up in hours/minutes).

- Develop a new process to ensure regular contact with long-term clients by (date).

  Measures: no client goes longer than xx months without personal contact; no clients missed; every client has face-to-face contact at least every x years; client feedback; new business from long-term clients.

You can see that to produce these more qualitative objectives, you need to be creative and think really hard about what the meaningful measures are. A common mistake is to fall back on crudely quantifiable numbers, but these often aren't a meaningful measure of what you are really after.

For example, when I started as a company training manager in my early career, my initial set of measures, given to me by my manager, were:

- Number and frequency of training courses per year.
- Number and level of employees trained.
- Number and variety of courses attended per employee.
- Scores obtained on the end-of-course evaluation survey.

>>>

Are these really a meaningful measure of how effectively I was doing my job? Not really. By the time I left the company a few years later, the measures were:

- Agreed learning objectives met (these were agreed between participants and their managers before the training programme).

- Changes in participants' behaviour.

- Feedback from participants' managers, immediately following the training and six months and one year on.

- Improvements in participants' measurable results (i.e. they met or exceeded their own performance objectives as a result of the training).

- All stakeholders' satisfaction (measured by asking them).

All these standards are not as easy to measure as the crudely quantifiable list given to me by my manager, but they are a much more accurate readout of how effectively I was doing my job as training manager.

Some hints

- If you know quality work when you see it, then there *is* a set of criteria you are using. You may not be consciously aware of it, nor immediately able to articulate it, but it is there.

- With sufficient rigour, you can always come up with a list of clearly observable or measurable behaviour or result statements.

- Don't fall into the trap of using crude numerical measurements just because they are easier.

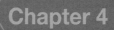

Chapter 4

Are you managing or operating?

Working communication skill no. 4:
managing your time

Chapter 4 – Are you managing or operating?

- 'I'm an engineer, software expert, accountant (fill in the gap) – I didn't sign up for this (people management).'
- 'I never get any time to do my job without someone interrupting to talk to me.'
- 'It's all touchy-feely – you're either good at that stuff or you're not.'
- 'I just want to get on with my job.'
- 'I need peace and quiet to work. Why do my team need to talk things over and ask questions all the time?'

These are common complaints from highly expert people – teachers, doctors, scientists, engineers, and many more – who have been so good at their specialist jobs that they seem to have found themselves at the top of their particular tree. But they discover the job seems to have changed; it no longer appears to be about focusing on and developing their specialism. They have acquired a team to manage, paperwork to do, and meetings about the running of the organisation to attend, when all they really want to do is get on with the job. How often do you find yourself thinking these thoughts or something like them?

One of the ironies of organisational life is often that the better you are at your specialism, the more likely it is that you'll be moved up the organisational ladder to a level where you are in charge of others doing that work. You may even find that there's no real call for you to do your specialist work in any depth any more. What's going on?

And even if you love your specialism and would like to spend the rest of your working life focusing on it, unless you work for one of a handful of enlightened organisations, the likelihood is that you are slowly realising that unless you accept a shift to management, your status in the organisation, and your salary, will never rise beyond a certain point.

The prevailing mindset

Asma is an associate director of a financial advisory company in the City of London that relies heavily on the specialists in its highly regarded investment department for the development of the innovative products, investment opportunities and financial solutions it offers its wealthy clients.

Asma is an investment analyst by training and her company has always relied on her and her colleagues to be consistently up to date with developments in worldwide markets and to come up with creative new approaches and solutions. All through her professional career, from university onwards, she has relied on having time and peace to do the research and reading she needs to do. Only then does she feel she can provide the highest quality advice for the financial advisers in the company to pass on to their external clients. She's done this work very well: so well that the company has rewarded her by putting her in charge of a team of four investment analysts with a team administrator, and given her the job title of associate director. She was initially delighted.

But now, from Asma's point of view, it's all gone wrong. She no longer has five or six hours in the day to read, research and think about the complex material she enjoys. It seems that somebody always needs her advice, or to check something or to resolve an issue in the office. She resents the interruptions and is beginning to get irritated with her team. She expects them to get on with their work without interrupting her, and cannot understand why they seem to need to talk about it all the time.

One thing Asma's missed of course is the mindset we discussed in Chapter 1 – her team, by definition, are no longer a group of individuals, tucked away on their own doing their research in isolation. They work in an office together, under a team leader (Asma), inside an investment department, which itself is part of a larger organisation. They have become an organism – a hive – and the bees in a hive need to communicate up, down and across the hierarchy, to maintain their relationships, to organise their work and to ensure that each of them is doing exactly the work they should be for the whole organism to survive and thrive. What sounds to Asma like insecurity (they keep asking her and each other questions) and chit-chat (they swap information and ideas on what they are working on, so they keep the team informed) is actually the sound of a busy working team doing its job.

And the other thing she's missed is that because she has accepted a role as team leader of this little organism, her entire role has by definition changed. Asma still sees herself as an expert, a specialist operator entirely focused on practising her professional specialism, who has been rewarded with promotion. But she hasn't understood that accepting the promotion has been taken as tacit acceptance that she understands that her role needs to change. Her team needs a custodian – she hasn't recognised it, and nobody made this clear to her when she accepted the job.

She's still trying to do the old job, and spend as much time as she used to in deepening her professional knowledge and expertise, and coming up with innovative new ideas. Management to Asma feels like an irritating interruption to what she still thinks of as her day job.

A more productive mindset

What's needed of Asma now is that she reduces the time and focus on continuously developing her own knowledge and expertise, and learns to deliver the same quality service via her management of her team of up-and-coming young specialists. In fact, their training and development as future leaders of the organisation is a crucial part of her new role.

Nobody explained this to Asma when she was promoted because it's a hugely misunderstood mechanism in growing organisations. Significant numbers of senior leaders in larger organisations try to hang on to the day job they entered the organisation to do, whether it's getting their sleeves rolled up and their hands dirty helping to sort out something on the factory floor, or shutting the door on their team to get time to get on with the job in peace. That's their understanding of how career development works, so they are simply managing their organisations in the way they themselves were managed. They are rewarding specialists like Asma with promotion with very little real grasp of the true magnitude of the change she will need to embrace.

Like Asma, what all these leaders have missed is that their whole job needs to change its focus as they rise to the top of their organisation and become responsible for the performance, experience and career development of more junior team members. Management is now an increasingly large part of the day job. This vital role is not one that you can carry out with half your mind during the (non-existent) spare time you have after you've finished a full-time specialist role – it's a crucial role in its own right, and deserves to have time and attention paid to it.

Coming to this realisation is difficult in today's world, because very few people are given the luxury of becoming a manager completely. In the old days, we all fantasise, you got your promotion to management, you got a new office, and an assistant, and instantly your changed status was fully understood by everyone around you. (I'm not sure this is completely true, by the way, but it forms such an important part of literature and film that we've all grown up with a rather old-fashioned view of how business, organisations and management used to work.) If it were the case, you would be able to sit back, delegate the specialist work (assuming you want to let it go) and concentrate your full attention on nurturing and growing your little stable of up-and-coming youngsters.

These days, however, with leaner, flatter organisation structures, and information technology that means we have to do our own administration and documentation, all of us have to learn to continue to do the day job, to the standards we have become so proud of, *alongside* managing a team of people who need our support in delivering to similar standards and in learning to work well with each other. It means we have to learn to dual-track in our minds, to manage our time more effectively, and really confront ourselves and our motivation for wanting promotion in the first place.

Figure 2 shows what happens.

Figure 2 – Are you managing or operating?

As you rise up the organisation, the balance between operating and managing shifts. When you started, you might have had the luxury of spending 90 per cent of your time and focus on your research, your software development, your teaching or your work in the lab. By the time you are a middle or senior manager the balance should be shifting, so that you are spending 50 per cent of your time or more on managing. (What's included in this? Read the next chapter to start to understand this better.)

Even very senior managers these days still don't have the luxury of giving up the day job completely – almost nobody does in the vast majority of the middle-sized organisations we are talking about here. We all have to find a way of learning to be a manager and leader alongside being an operator.

So, as you become a senior manager in most organisations, your focus needs to shift away from your specialism and towards this thing called management. You don't have to let go of your expertise, nor your standards. But if you are to do the job properly, you do have to learn how to deliver the same expertise and standards *through other people*.

You have to become the head teacher who inspires her team to the standards of impeccability and professionalism that she showed as a young teacher in the classroom herself. Or the former software engineer who as company MD learns enough about marketing, finance and people management to turn his company into a world-beater. But if you are resisting the realisation and resenting every minute spent away from the day job, like Asma, you are missing a crucial truth – *you are no longer doing your job properly*.

The day job, at this level of management, is a mix. If you try to continue to put in the time and effort you used to into your area of expertise, you're either neglecting the managing part of your job, or you're hanging on to your specialist work and ending up trying to do a double job. It's no wonder many people in the higher levels of organisational leadership feel overwhelmed and overloaded.

And if you embrace management and neglect your former day job, you are equally not doing your job properly. It's probably true to say though that not many people embrace management with both arms – they like the status and the money the promotion brings, but relatively few people really understand the full implications of making the move. It's more usual that people accept the new role in name only, focus their efforts where they feel most comfortable, on their familiar specialism, and resent and resist spending time learning and practising professional management and communication skills. Managing gets pushed to the margins.

Clients say to me that they usually do their planning, their forecasting, their perfor-mance management and their thinking about organisational issues in the evenings and at weekends, 'because it's the only time I get when I can think about it properly'. This mindset gives away their assumption that their specialism is the real day job. Management is what you do when you can find the time. And that's those who even try to do it at all; many of them just leave it, because it's difficult, they resent the time spent on it and because they don't think they have the skills, until it all blows up in their face and they have to do something or they'll get taken to court.

Do you even really want the job?

When you really think about it, if you get the implications of what I'm saying, you might have to give some thought to whether you really want that senior management position after all. If, like Asma, you really love reading and researching investment and market knowledge for four to six hours a day, you should be doing a research job. And if you love the buzz, the variety and the achievement of classroom teach-ing, then you should remain a classroom teacher. If at senior level you still insist on trying to keep your hand in, a crucial job – management – is not getting done well enough, or sometimes at all. It's not about indulging your preferences: there's a job to be done at senior level, and too few people are treating it as a specialism in its own right.

'But', I hear you say, 'then I won't get the status or the pay that come with progression up the organisation.' True. You may not – there are very few organisations that have recognised this and made alternative career paths available to specialists that allow them the satisfaction of progression without taking them away from their area of expertise. But you'll be a happier and more fulfilled person – and you'll make space for someone else to come through who loves managing others to deliver the specialist work, and nurturing and growing people in their jobs. Your organism needs a custodian, and if it isn't going to be you, you had better make room for somebody better suited than you to do the job that needs doing. Everyone benefits.

What if you really accept that, while you used to be a professional specialist, you'd actually quite welcome a change in role, and you are now willing to spend time and effort becoming a great manager and leader of people?

How do you apply this mindset to your leadership?

1. Take an honest look at yourself. Are you a specialist, better suited to being an operator than a manager? Should you stay in that role, even if it means looking for more suitable work elsewhere, and maybe accepting less pay?
2. Are you willing to make the shift, but worry that you don't have the skills? Read on.
3. Choose. Make the choice to embrace the change – or not. If it's not for you, step aside. Don't stick around and try to do both badly – it's bad for you, and it's bad for your organisation and the people who work in it.
4. If you do decide to take on the job, what split of time/focus on managing to operating will be appropriate at your level in the organisation, and taking into account the capabilities of your team? It should not be less than 50:50 – that's two and a half days managing per week.

Get training – you didn't get to be a specialist in the day job without years of training. Why should management and leadership skills be any different? Start by reading the rest of this book.

*The key is not to prioritize what's on your schedule,
but to schedule your priorities.*

Stephen Covey

Here's an example of how time management works:

A trainer working with a group placed a large glass jar on a table. He produced about a dozen fist-sized rocks and put them one at a time into the jar.

When the jar was filled to the top and no more rocks would fit inside, he asked, 'Is this jar full?' Everyone in the group said 'Yes'. 'Really?' he asked. 'Let's see.' He then pulled out a bucket of gravel. Putting some gravel into the jar, he shook it, so that the pieces of gravel moved into the spaces between the big rocks.

He asked again, 'Is the jar full?' The group was catching on quickly. 'No', they said.

He then brought out a bucket of sand. As he poured the sand in, it went into the spaces left between the rocks and the gravel. He finished and asked again, 'Is this jar full?' 'Probably not', someone answered.

'Excellent', he replied. And he took a jug of water and poured it in until the jar was filled to the brim.

What's the point of this example? What would have happened if he had put the sand and gravel in first? That's right – unless you put the big rocks in first, you won't get them in at all. Or if you apply this to your business, make sure you plan enough time to work on the big issues you face or the smaller stuff will take over. This will then leave you with no time to fit those important issues in.

What are the big rocks in your life and work? How do you make the decision as to what to put in your jar – your diary – first?

Table 3 shows a way of making the decision – and making sure that your diary doesn't just fill up with the sand, leaving no room for anything else.

>>>

Table 3 – What to do first and how to fit in the important stuff

	Not urgent	Urgent
Important **(Key result areas)**	B Block time in your diary	A Do it now
Not important **(Not key result areas)**	D Dump it	C Clearing house – re-sort into A, B or D

You can see Table 3 balances the *urgency* against the *importance* of the task at hand. Important tasks address your key result areas, and may or may not be urgent. Non-important tasks address other areas, and likewise may or may not be urgent. This gives you a way of sorting tasks in your daily work.

ABCD scheduling

If a task is important *and* urgent, no question, it's an A priority task – just do it. If it's not important – that is it doesn't address your key result areas, and it's not urgent – don't do it. Just dump it.

Now, I realise this raises the question of what to do if it's not important to you, but is to someone else. This is where you will need to learn to negotiate effectively with others over what's important and not important in your business, and you may even need to steel yourself and say 'no' (appropriately, of course) to a few people. There's advice later in this book on how to do these things. But most importantly of all, don't just do the task because someone else has told you it's urgent. Learn to make your own decisions, based on the needs of the business and what you know is important and urgent in your own job.

If a task is important, but not urgent, it's a big rock – schedule it in your diary in sensible-sized chunks, based on what you know the normal demands of your job are. Don't block out four hours in one day if you know you never have long stretches without something you will need to respond to. Break the important task into shorter chunks and schedule an hour or so at a time. It's fairer to your colleagues not to just disappear for long stretches of time, and they are more likely to respect your need to shut yourself away if you are reasonable in your scheduling. And even an enormous task will eventually get done if you schedule an hour a week – provided you honour the schedule. >>>

If you are not sure, or the task doesn't seem to fall clearly into A, B or D, then it's a C. Use C as a clearing house. Place all these emails, job requests, etc. in one place and give them some thought, or go back to the originator and ask them whether the task is urgent or important. Only when you are satisfied that it fits your criteria should you schedule the task for action. Sometimes, just taking a short time to think about it makes the situation clearer – it either goes away, or its urgency or importance becomes much clearer, and the answer is obvious.

Scheduling your management tasks

If you're one of those people I mentioned in the last chapter who leaves your planning, forecasting, performance management and thinking about organisational issues to evenings and weekends, 'because it's the only time I get when I can think about it properly', managing your time in this way is the answer. These activities are usually B priority tasks – important, but rarely urgent. Leaving them to evenings and weekends reveals that you are allowing your normal working week to be overrun by urgent and probably by operational tasks. All conscientious senior leaders do some thinking and work in their personal time, but to do it regularly as a matter of course is a sign of failed prioritisation and time management. Schedule these tasks, in bite-sized chunks, into your normal working hours, and train your colleagues to respect these sessions. After all, you are simply doing your proper job as their leader and manager.

Take time to manage time

You may by now be realising that managing your time effectively takes some time – and that's true. The most effective people in the world manage their time consciously and continuously. They allocate time to sorting out the diary – and the busier they are, *the more time they spend doing it*.

This process of getting off the back foot onto the front foot with time management is horribly counter-intuitive. You will want to just get on with something – anything – to reduce the load. But if you don't spend time at the beginning of each day, and again during the day, to organise and reorganise how you manage your time, you'll end up spending it in one of two ways. Either you'll be seduced by *urgency*, and knock off lots of urgent tasks, only some of which will be important. Or you'll be attracted by reducing the *quantity* of tasks and process lots of tasks that are neither urgent nor important, but give you a little thrill of satisfaction because you can knock them off your list. >>>

But if you discipline yourself to start questioning and managing how you spend your time, by blocking out time in your diary to do the big rocks – the B priority tasks – you'll be pleasantly surprised at how much this reduces your guilt and anxiety at never getting round to them. And the other stuff, the sand and gravel, will carry on happening anyway and, strangely, seems to fit in around the edges.

Some hints

- Delegate as much as possible – if you don't have a lot of people working for you directly, then look at passing work to other departments, temps, external suppliers, interns, volunteers. But only pass important work – don't clutter them up with unimportant stuff either.

- Some tasks just need to be dumped. Reduce the proportion of your time spent on *non-important* tasks – if in doubt just don't do them. If they were actually more important than you thought, they'll resurface.

- Find ways of automating tasks – time spent on finding the right hard- and software can be time well spent. Use planning tools – Outlook, project management software, reminder lists with alarms, whatever works for you.

- Find ways of dealing with constantly recurring problems – don't fix, re-engineer.

- Eighty per cent of your time should be spent on 20 per cent of your tasks – the key result areas.

- Make time for yourself, to manage your time as well as for important tasks, and respect it as you would a meeting with somebody else. Tell team members, managers, colleagues, customers, family and friends the best times to contact you and train them to respect those times.

- For scheduled tasks close the door, hang up a sign, book a meeting room, switch off your phone and train people not to disturb you unless it's a dire emergency. Don't automatically do these tasks at home outside core working hours – this is a failure in time management.

- When people call in or telephone unexpectedly, always find out how long they need. It may be more convenient to arrange to see or call them back later. In other words, apply the ABCD rule on the spot. Discourage people from starting important conversations on the hoof without booking time first – and don't do this to others either.

>>>

- When requesting information or work to be done, ask for it a little earlier than you really need it. When estimating the time needed to do a job, always allow extra for unforeseen events.
- When given a task, always find out when it is needed by, and how important the other person thinks it is so you can plan priorities, or even consider rejecting the work.
- Have only one task on your desk or place of work at a time. Make sure you have all the information you need to complete it, and finish it fully before starting the next task.
- Train others to use the ABCD system too.

Chapter 5

Maintaining the balance

Working communication skill no. 5:
listening effectively

Chapter 5 – Maintaining the balance

- 'I've restructured the team, but they still don't seem motivated.'
- 'People are still complaining they don't feel part of things, yet we've spent a fortune on the new branding exercise.'
- 'We updated and published the new company values but the dodgy behaviour still hasn't changed.'
- 'What does it take to get people fired up? What more could we have done?'

What *does* it take to get people fired up? You've taken on board that your organisation needs to be managed as a whole, and that you're the one to do it. You've let go of much of the specialist work you used to do and delegated it to some bright young trainees. You've been on a management skills programme, employed every skill in your new kitbag and done everything you can think of, but the buzz still isn't happening. What on earth is missing?

The prevailing mindset

Daniel is a senior director in a large global name property company. Part of its strategy over the last couple of years has been to bring in-house a service – facilities management – which hitherto it had not offered its clients. Directors believe that this will enable them to offer clients a full end-to-end management service for the properties they supply them with. The strategy has been to take over facilities management functions lock, stock and barrel from larger clients and then, without initially making any major changes to staff or standards, to offer the service back to those clients under the new owner's brand. It's a tricky cultural change for the employees, who have often worked for one company for many years and identified with that company. Now, without anything in their daily life changing very much, they work for a different organisation, with different conditions, norms and culture – and all without changing their colleagues or their place of work.

In a conversation, Daniel confessed, 'I'm at my wits' end. I've changed the management structure, their terms and conditions, their contracts, put them on the company bonus scheme. We've had regular meetings to discuss work in progress and establish relationships with us here at the new company. We've even changed all their email addresses and their screensavers. But there's still no buzz. What more can I do?'

I suggested gently that none of those changes really addressed the concerns, fears and anxieties attendant for most people on a major change of employer. Even if the move is positive, it takes time for people to buy in and to welcome change – and they need space to express some of those anxieties and talk themselves round to a more enthusiastic frame of mind. Brow furrowed, Daniel listened carefully to what I had to say, and I thought he seemed to understand. Then slowly and thoughtfully he said, 'Hmm. I think I see what you mean. I wonder, do you think it would help if we put them in a uniform?'

Daniel is typical of many senior leaders. Because all his education and training has been in the concrete skills of data collection and analysis, factual reporting, re-engineering, structuring, organising and control, those are the skills he naturally tries to employ when facing an issue like motivating his new team, and generating enthusiasm and buzz. Even the management skills programme he attended recently focused heavily on the regulatory and financial aspects of running a company. Notice that everything he's tried is concrete – new systems, screen savers, terms and conditions, organisation structure and contracts.

While these are all vital and necessary aspects of managing people in terms of good practice and company governance, none of them really addresses the personal and emotional needs of a group of employees uprooted from one place of work and dumped into another. Initially of course, they'll be relieved to hear that their jobs are safe and their terms of employment haven't changed too much. They'll welcome good administration (new email addresses, terms and conditions, etc.) and integration with the new company's infrastructure. And the information and background they have received about the new company at the management meetings will have given them a useful context for their new jobs.

But Daniel's new team are likely to be feeling a range of emotions, anywhere from excitement and enthusiasm to apprehension and anxiety. Nowhere has he consciously designed and provided an outlet for this. So they are much more likely to talk among themselves, put on a brave face and quietly get on with their work, than to tell him how they are feeling. Only if they really get the chance and a well-managed space to share their full range of feelings with each, their new colleagues and Daniel, will they begin to tap into the creativity, the excitement and the ideas that Daniel means by buzz.

And notice that when trying to get his head around the tricky concepts of giving people space, listening to them and talking about the environment he's trying to create, Daniel's knee-jerk reaction is to revert to a *tangible* thing to do – 'perhaps if we put them in a uniform, they'll feel more buzz'. It's a natural reaction for someone with a conventional Western world business background – but to be successful in generating buzz and fun, loyalty, creativity and enthusiasm, Daniel is going to have to learn to harness different skills from the ones that have got him to where he is today.

A more productive mindset

It will help here if you accept that there are two distinct sets of things to manage in yourself, others, the team and the business. Look at Figure 3.

Figure 3 – Intangible and tangible – the management balance

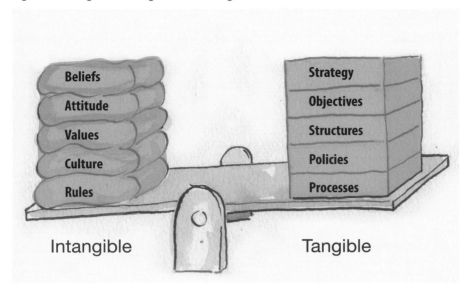

On the right-hand end of the balance, there are all the things you notice and instinctively recognise need managing. If you, like most of the business leaders I meet, are like Daniel, these will usually be relatively tangible things like systems and structures, because that's the way you've been taught to think. And you, like him, will very probably have many of the skills (organising, re-engineering, administering, data collection and recording, and so on) needed to manage these things. These are obvious – they are *what* you do to build a stable, safe and legal organisation, and you may well lose employees, upset your customers or even get prosecuted if you don't make an adequate job of managing them.

But at the other end of the balance are things like attitudes, values, beliefs and behaviour – *how* you do what you do. These are things you may not even notice, with your practical and concrete mindset, until they go badly wrong and demand your attention – and actually you aren't usually prosecuted for managing these badly. It's for this reason that I am very often called in when communication needs repairing and relationships have broken down – the very time that feelings are running too high and people are feeling too hurt, angry and emotional to be able to have a straightforward conversation to resolve what went wrong.

One reason this happens is that people like Daniel have learned to regard things at this end of the balance as a minefield, and resolving them as a black art best left to experts like myself. The trouble is that dealing with breakdowns in attitudes, values and behaviour is not hard, but it does require skills that perhaps don't come quite so naturally to you, like listening, exploring, sharing, communicating. These situations need to be nipped in the bud early on, before everybody is too upset to talk to each other. Then you really will need an expert.

Not only are these skills easy to learn, so that you can handle most situations yourself before they turn into a crisis, but it's your job to learn these skills and handle this type of situation. This isn't a complicated and highly technical area of skill and expertise best left to the experts. It's a crucial part of your role as a leader and manager of the people in your organisation. You are accountable for the values and attitudes of your organisation, and for how they are expressed in the behaviour of the people who work for you: it's called your organisation's culture, and if you are not managing it with as much rigour as you employ to manage your finances, *you are only doing half your job*.

Different skills and different outcomes

It may help here if you recognise that it is possible to manage the things on the left-hand end of the balance with *as much rigour and specificity* as you employ to manage the things at the right-hand end. However, the skills and the metrics you use will be different.

Once you recognise that it is possible to manage the 'intangible' with as much rigour as the 'tangible', then it simply becomes a matter of assessing to what degree you have the necessary skills (if required, getting some training in these) and learning how to create the measurement systems you will need (see Table 4).

Table 4 – Skills and metrics for managing intangible and tangible aspects of your organisation

	Intangible	**Tangible**
Skills	• Listening • Questioning • Facilitating • Giving feedback • Meeting management • Time management • Empathy	• Data collection • Data analysis • Reporting • Re-engineering • Structuring • Organising • Control
Metrics	• Observable behaviour • Feedback (formal and informal, 360, employee surveys, etc.) • Decisions made • Actions implemented • Time, cost, duplication saved	• Statistics • Numbers • Money • Variances • Ratios • Rates

Once you have fully taken on board that managing your organisation properly requires that you manage both ends of the balance with equal rigour and skill, you will need to develop a feel for what needs handling at any given time, and for how to handle it. Ask yourself the question, 'What does the business need right now?' The answer to this may be more subtle than you think at first, and tends to move from one end of the balance to the other and back again as situations arise and change.

Some issues are going to be clear-cut. If the production line stops, then an engineering solution will probably be appropriate. If there's a clear-cut case of sexual harassment, then a disciplinary process followed by dismissal will be the right answer.

But if production is mysteriously down one quarter? Or the team seems to spend a lot of time making mistakes and blaming other people? The answer probably won't lie at the right-hand end of the balance. Yet it's surprising to me how often production managers resort to setting the target higher in the belief this will resolve the problem. Or the team leader writes a new process and enforces it in the hope that the number of mistakes will fall.

In one of the most famous experiments in early management theory, Elton Mayo conducted a series of experiments at the Hawthorne factory of the Western Electric Company in Chicago. He isolated two groups of women workers and studied the effect on their productivity levels of changing factors such as lighting and working conditions.

He expected to see productivity levels decline as lighting or other conditions became progressively worse.

What he actually discovered surprised him: whatever the change in lighting or working conditions, even if they became worse, the productivity levels of the workers remained the same or even improved. From this, Mayo concluded that workers are best motivated by:

- Better communication between managers and workers (workers were consulted over the experiments and also had the opportunity to give feedback).
- Greater manager involvement in employees' working lives (workers responded to the increased level of attention they were receiving).
- Working in groups or teams (workers did not previously regularly work in teams).

So very often the answer will lie in talking and listening to people and involving them in finding solutions that may not immediately be apparent. This is not a soft option; it's a crucial leadership skill. You will find over time that your focus will naturally shift from one side to the other of the balance and back again. You'll spend some time installing new systems and processes, then realise that you've lost the hearts and minds and have to do some talking and listening to bring people along with you. Or you'll have a big push on the new company values, then have to bring people back to a clear focus on targets and results.

Of course it's best if you learn to integrate the two ends and run them concurrently as far as possible. So alongside the introduction of your new production control system, instead of waiting for the outside consultants to finish their work and present the new system as a fait accompli, you include people in meetings to share their frustrations, implement the system and resolve problems throughout the installation.

The process of involving them in a structured way may in itself motivate the production staff to find that extra bit of speed, or the team to sort out its error rate by itself – and if the answer is to be found in increased targets or a bit of engineering wizardry, then they'll find that out too.

Remember that your job as the leader of a larger 2G organisation is to be a custodian, not to find all the answers yourself (nor to hire outside consultants to supply state-of-the-art solutions for you). The bees in the hive actually do know how to run the system. They may just need you to show interest and listen, then stand back and empower them to find their own answers.

How do you apply this mindset to your leadership?

- Recognise that you will usually assume that the issue, and its solution, lie somewhere on the right-hand side of the balance.
- Recognise also that your instincts will usually be to focus on tangible things you can do to fix issues in your organisation.
- Start to hold back on supplying solutions to your teams, and create multiple platforms and structures – regular ideas meetings, problem-solving groups, one-to-one meetings with managers, for example – for them to have conversations among themselves to resolve problems and tweak the organisational culture as it grows. Without a space specifically to focus on this, all meetings tend naturally to gravitate towards operational issues.
- If you do involve outside experts, make sure they share your belief that the people affected don't just need a say in the solution (the dreaded focus group), but actually have to be *part* of its creation and implementation.
- Get yourself and your key managers trained in questioning, listening, meeting facilitation and problem-solving skills, and use these skills consciously in everyday work.
- Use trained facilitators to get the best out of meetings and allow people to share and develop their ideas without being unconsciously closed down by task-focused meeting leaders.

- Recognise that doing it this way may take a little longer, but you'll end up with engaged and motivated people and solutions that last – and you won't have had to come up with all the answers yourself.

Isn't that better than short-term fixes and the stress of knowing that it's all down to you at the end of the day?

Most people do not listen with the intent to understand; they listen with the intent to reply.

Stephen R. Covey

How well do you listen? Have you in fact ever thought about whether there is any way to listen other than the one that comes naturally to you? I didn't – until I encountered the idea of active listening and realised just how little I actually engaged with the people I was talking to and what they were saying.

This is how most people listen:

You: 'What did you do at the weekend?'
Them: 'I went hang-gliding.'
You: 'Wow, that's interesting. I went ballooning.'
Them: 'Yes, I loved the feeling of being out in the open air and up high, so you can see everything.'

>>>

You: 'Oh, so did I. Ballooning's great for that – you can see for miles.'
Them: 'Well, hang-gliding's great for that too – and you can control where you're going…'

Can you see what's happening? *You* asked *them* what they did at the weekend, and every time they try to tell you, you talk about what you did.

Listen to people talking around you and you'll quickly realise it's almost as if they are having parallel monologues – talking about broadly similar topics. Even if they are arguing, they aren't listening to the other's point of view; they're just waiting for them to take a breath, so they can share their own opinion. They're on the same track, but on separate rails – fairly close, but never together, stretching into the distance but never meeting.

So what is active listening?

Well, like every other skill in this book, it begins with a mindset shift. The prevailing mindset goes something like, 'I'm in this conversation to get my ideas and thoughts across. I'll wait for the minimum respectable amount of time [not everybody even does this, by the way] and then say my bit.'

A more productive mindset is, 'For at least half of this conversation, I'm going to make it my business to really listen to what the other person is saying, and try my hardest to set aside my own opinions and needs.'

Don't worry about this feeling unnatural and something of an effort – it is for most of us. The feeling is one of *choosing*: choosing to get off your rail for a specific period of time and go and sit with them on theirs. Listen to the conversation now:

You: 'What did you do at the weekend?'
Them: 'I went hang-gliding.'
You: 'Wow, that's interesting. What was that like?'

>>>

Them: 'Oh, I loved the feeling of being out in the open air and up high, so you can see everything.'

You: 'How did it feel?'

Them: 'Well, a bit scary at first, but I quickly got so fascinated by what I could see that I forgot to be frightened.'

You: 'Tell me more about what it was like…'

Can you see that listening this way is far more likely to help them to open up and tell you more about how they felt? You might even learn something you didn't know, if you concentrate on listening to what they are saying rather than to yourself preparing your response.

So you need to *choose* to listen, and discipline your thoughts when they threaten to draw you off the other person's rail onto your own again. At first, you will probably find you can only do this for very short periods of time – two or three sentences, if you're lucky. But the principle is what's important – you are listening to them, with the aim of giving them your full attention for as long as you possibly can.

The extreme example of really listening to another is in counselling, therapy or pure coaching, where the therapist or coach is trained never to intrude their own opinions or thoughts at all. However, this is not practicable for most people, nor really appropriate for a business setting, so how can you train yourself to listen more actively for at least some of the time, perhaps when you are coaching or interviewing, or just want to build a better relationship with somebody at work?

Active listening

A big surprise for most people is to realise that asking questions doesn't necessarily make you a good listener. Actually, if you think about it, asking questions, however good you are, is actually coming from your own rail – you are thinking about what you need to know and what information you'd like to find out. So how can you listen actively, and stay with them on their rail?

Well, you reflect back to them what they have said. Ask a question to get them going, then when they pause for breath, confirm what they have said by repeating it back to them, as closely as possible in their own words. It may feel

>>>

a little odd to you, but I promise you, most people are so delighted to know you really got what they said that they'll just rush on with the next thing they wanted to say. You'll know you got it right, if after each time you repeat back their words to them, they say, 'Yes, and...' and they're off again.

If they never seem to take a breath, and you get worried that you won't be able to remember it all accurately when the time comes for you to reflect back what they've said, this is the one time in communication that you *can* interrupt. Usually, we interrupt to drag someone off their rail onto ours, and this is perceived as irritating and rude. If, however, you interrupt to help someone clarify their thoughts or expand on something they've said, not only will they not think you're being rude, they'll actually find it flattering and helpful. Use phrases like, 'Hold on, say that again', or 'Let me just say back to you what I think you're trying to say', and they'll happily repeat what they've said for your benefit. You're staying on their rail, you see. Again, you'll know you've got it right if they say, 'Yes, and...' and rush onwards again.

Be careful not to use this technique to twist what they say to make it match what you want to hear – this is a not-so-subtle attempt to get them onto your rail, and feels manipulative to the speaker. You are trying to build trust and a relationship, and can only do this if you genuinely want to understand what they are really trying to say.

A good tip, if you find this difficult at first, is to use phrases like, 'So if I understand you right, what you are saying is...', or, 'Let me see if I've got exactly what you're saying. You said...' You can also say, 'Tell me more...', or, 'Go on...' You'll find that nobody will mind being interrupted for you to feed back their own words to them. They'll know you are really trying to understand and will find it flattering and empowering. Very few of us have the experience of being listened to properly by others, and it's refreshing when we do.

Some hints

- Having made the choice to listen to someone, use appropriate body language: lean towards them, make eye contact, put away anything you are looking at or holding and encourage them by nodding and smiling from time to time.

>>>

- Make noises, especially if listening on the phone. It's very disconcerting talking into a vacuum – we are so used to being interrupted that you do need to make it clear that you are still listening even though you are not chipping in.

- Hold off questioning for as long as possible in the conversation – appropriate use of body language, encouraging noises and reflecting will keep a person going longer than you would think possible – and you are more likely to find out something you don't already know if you avoid questions.

- If you do use questions, keep them as open as possible. Questions beginning with 'how', 'why' and 'what' tend to lead to more open responses than 'yes/no' questions and ones beginning with 'who', 'when' and 'where'. See 'Working communication skill no. 7', p101, for more on questioning.

- A really good test of your listening and a chance to practise, though very difficult, is to *really* listen to someone whose views you disagree with. Don't disagree *or agree* with them, just try to get absolutely clear on what they believe and why they believe it, and reflect it back to them without twisting their words – or sounding incredulous.

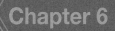

Chapter 6

You're their leader, not their friend

Working communication skill no. 6:
how to be assertive

Chapter 6 – You're their leader, not their friend

- 'They don't treat me like one of the gang any more.'
- 'I had a friendly chat with Joe over lunch the other day, but his behaviour still hasn't changed – I don't understand it.'
- 'I've treated them just like a big family – and this is the thanks I get.'
- 'People take advantage of my good nature – I'm so disappointed.'

Have you been disappointed that as you've risen up your organisation, you no longer feel you are accepted as one of the crowd? Do you even feel a little lonely? Are you constantly surprised that people don't seem to want to do the things you try to persuade them to do, even though you bend over backwards to be generous to them and create a friendly atmosphere? Well, there's good news, and there's bad news (depending on your point of view). You *can* create an environment in which people are happy and motivated and do the things that will help your business grow and thrive … *but*, if you do it right, you will very probably be regarded, in most cases, not as their friend, but as their leader.

The prevailing mindset

Maria has run a successful high-end fashion shop in a pretty market town in the Cotswolds for 25 years, and many of her staff have been with her for much of that time. She's a talented designer and fashion buyer and the business is thriving, despite the economic ups and downs of recent years.

But something doesn't feel right. Some team members are complaining and gossiping behind Maria's back, sometimes even complaining to customers about how Maria manages them. Even those who don't complain about the management often spend a lot of time talking to each other in front of customers about their own lives and issues, even drawing customers into the gossip. Jealousy and rivalries between some of the longer-standing team members have begun to sour the working atmosphere.

Maria is a warm, kind woman who has always tried to treat people as friends, resolving their issues by giving them a shoulder to cry on when necessary, and where possible giving them what they want in terms of shift patterns and time off. Now she's finding it almost impossible to run the business to meet everybody's needs and preferences, and the customers are starting to comment on the atmosphere when they come into the shop.

Maria feels almost bullied by her staff, especially as when she tries to resolve issues there is always somebody who doesn't like the solution and sulks. She is at her wits' end as to how to deal with the situation, and worse, she's now finding that she's also getting irritated and angry with people.

In fact, they are all falling into the same trap – they are trying to have *social* relationships with each other. I have to laugh when people say to me, 'I believe in treating people as I would treat my friends/family', because most friends and family don't *work* together – and look what very often happens when they do!

In the prevailing mindset, most people believe that they use two sets of skills at work: their technical skills (fashion designer, IT specialist, engineer, architect, teacher…) and their social skills (getting on with people, communication, organising themselves…). Their mindset looks like Figure 4.

Figure 4 – The prevailing mindset

My technical skills	**My social skills**

'Skills I think I need to be effective at work'

These are the leaders who say to me, 'Oh we do a lot of team building – we have a pizza evening at least once a month.' Or, 'Yes, I have regular meetings with my team members – I take each of them out for a beer on their own as often as I can so we can have a chat.'

What on earth for? You're not their mate; you're their organisation's leader. I would rather see you directing and leading your organisation – taking care of its finances, making sure it's ahead of the game in its market and providing it with good governance. Your employees don't have these skills: you do (hopefully), and they rely on you to keep their hive happy and healthy so they can do their jobs. If you do spend time talking with your team members – and I certainly believe you should – it should be to talk with them (not in a bar) about where the organisation is going and help them to understand, and be inspired by, how they can make the best contribution to this.

These are the things I would expect of a company director. Don't you think there's a set of skills missing in the above diagram?

A more productive mindset

There's another whole category of skills you need to master if you are to make and maintain good working relationships and take care of and nurture a healthy hive, whether you are the lowliest intern or the boss of the whole organisation. And it helps if everybody from the top to the bottom has some of the same core skills, with a good understanding of how these need to develop as you take more and more responsibility for the whole organisation. These are *working communication* skills: professional communication and management skills. Though there are obviously overlaps, working communication skills go way beyond the normal social skills you use to negotiate everyday life.

This mindset looks more like Figure 5.

Figure 5 – A more productive mindset

My technical skills	Working communication skills	My social skills

'Skills I actually need to be effective at work'

Some groups of colleagues like to socialise together as well as to work together. It's very easy in this situation to assume that because you all get on very well with each other you will always work well together. Actually you may well work very harmoniously with people at work who have become your friends – until something goes wrong. You've only got to look at the complicated situations that arise when there are misunderstandings or conflicts in families or groups of friends to see how unsuited this mode of communication usually is to resolving tricky situations. It's then that the value of working communication skills and processes really comes to the fore.

This is so evident in the kinds of work situation that I am brought in to help with that I would go so far as to say that work groups who *aren't* friends and who don't choose to socialise together, very often work much more effectively together than those who do. It often comes as a nasty shock to groups who socialise well, when they hit a tricky patch and relationships break down. Normal everyday social skills don't help much when relationships are in breakdown, as they then discover to their cost.

In the absence of any assumptions about the rules and norms of getting on together, groups of people who aren't naturally friends have had to negotiate explicit agreements about how they want to work and communicate, and they have very often made a good job of this, precisely because they have had no other basis to rely on. This helps enormously when things get sticky, because they can fall back on these agreements, or call on their working communication skills to negotiate new agreements.

They are also not emotionally involved with each other – once you have become friends with others in your work group, it's easy for you to feel hurt if someone doesn't like your work, offended if your boss has to give you critical feedback or rejected if colleagues appear to be leaving you out.

So what are 'working communication skills'?

Take a look at Figure 6 for an idea of the kinds of skills I mean.

Figure 6 – Working communication skills

Technical skills	Working communications skills	Social Skills
• Professional skills • Manual skills • Industry knowledge • Working experience • ...	• Listening • Negotiating • Calling to account • Being accountable • Leadership • Providing and receiving service • ...	• Being a good friend • Taking care of people • Shared experience of life • Giving and receiving love • Having fun together • ...

It's pretty clear to most of us what our *technical* skills are – they are the ones we started learning in school and gradually specialised in more and more as we went through further education, apprenticeships or early workplace training. These are the skills you will have gained qualifications in, and studied through reading, training or college courses: you've probably spent more time honing these specific skills than any others. And because of this, you are probably more aware of your skills in this area than in either of the other two areas.

On the other hand, like most of us, you will have learned your *social* skills by absorption from your earliest days in your family and at school: you're probably barely aware of them as a body of skills at all. They seem to you like 'just the way I do things'. You've probably learned by trial and error what works and what doesn't, what makes you popular and what will lose you friends. Most of us are more or less good at social skills, and it rarely occurs to us to get any coaching or training in them. Even in our most important social relationships, we usually only get professional help when things have already gone wrong – the 'marriage guidance' approach to learning relationship skills.

But the area I am really interested in here is the middle box – *working communication skills*. These are the skills that will make most difference to your performance and satisfaction throughout your working life, and in particular to your effectiveness as a leader. Most people confuse these with day-to-day social skills, but it's rare that any of us really brings these skills home and uses them in our personal and family relationships. If you are very skilled in this area, it's true that bringing some of these skills to your social relationships could certainly enhance them. For example, *listening* better could only improve your relationship with your partner or with close friends, as could *negotiating* or being more personally *accountable*. Though you need to be careful – too much emphasis on calling your partner to account might not go down well!

The other way around – bringing social skills to work – doesn't always make for a happier environment or for a more productive working day. The ways in which we cement our social relationships, sharing confidences, chatting about our lives and playing games together, by definition take up a lot of time which at work really needs to be spent ensuring that the organisation and its purpose are being fulfilled.

I CAN TELL YOU LADY, I GOT GREAT PEOPLE SKILLS

This is not to say that you can't or shouldn't have fun at work – quite the opposite. Fun and enjoyment are essential to remaining motivated and producing creative, excellent work. But there are ways of achieving these without taking the winding, hit-or-miss approach that is part of the joy of developing a close friendship over time. Let's leave the pleasure of this for our social relationships, and look harder at how to achieve a similar level of enjoyment and professional closeness to others by employing the third set of skills.

One of the skills you will need to develop if you take this mindset on board is to make a clear distinction in your own mind, and in the minds of the people you are talking to or working with, as to whether you are operating as friends or as professional/work colleagues right now. Most of us end up with some people in our lives with whom we have both relationships: the colleague who over a long period has become more of a friend, or the partner you live *and* work with. It helps of course if the person you are communicating with understands the distinction too, but sometimes you will need to say, 'I can't chat right now, I have work to do. Why don't we meet for a catch-up after work?' Or you might have to give someone tricky feedback (if you're their manager), and for that period of time, step clearly and explicitly out of friend mode. Or at home in the evening with your partner, one of you might have to say to the other, 'Let's not keep discussing our plans for the business. Let's just put our feet up and be mates for this evening.' It's not easy – but it's an awful lot easier if you both understand this mindset and the clear distinction between friend mode and work mode. In fact, if you have this problem with somebody, start by explaining this concept to them – you'll be surprised at the difference it makes.

How do you apply this mindset to your leadership?

- Don't be afraid to be explicit about which mode you are in – it might seem a bit clinical at first, but it avoids those misunderstandings where one of you is being clipped and efficient and the other is hurt because they thought you were having a friendly chat.
- Learn to say 'no' when you need to work and someone else wants to chat, or accept a 'no' when you need a chat after working hours and your colleague/ friend is stuck in work mode.
- Set work time and space aside for work conversations – don't try to have them in the pub or over lunch. It sends mixed messages, at least until you are very skilled at drawing the distinction in your mindset and through your behaviour.
- Keep friendly chit-chat mostly to break times and after work, and keep it to a minimum in office space and within earshot of others at work.
- Be very careful about becoming a shoulder to cry on – this crosses the work/ personal boundary, and is difficult to withdraw from once you've started. As an organisation leader, ensure there are appropriate counselling and pastoral services to refer people to, and avoid getting sucked in to emotional support for your employees beyond the immediate crisis period.
- Being fair, objective and clear with people isn't the same as being nice to them. The first is your job. The second isn't. Don't be nasty – but do be fair, clear and objective.

The difference between successful people and really successful people is that really successful people say no to almost everything.

Warren Buffett

Have you ever wondered why you can react perfectly coolly, logically and reasonably with certain people and situations, while with other people or other apparently similar situations you are reduced to a stammering wreck – or towering fury?

Assuming that you agree with me that it would be better if you were able to act coolly, logically and reasonably in the vast majority of situations (perhaps excluding actual physical threat or with a person who is totally beyond rational conversation), then it's a good idea to examine what's going on in these situations.

Assertive, passive, aggressive

We call the cool, logical and reasonable response being *assertive*, and it can extend anywhere from quietly and courteously refusing to do something you don't want to do, right through to very strongly asserting your viewpoint or your wishes.

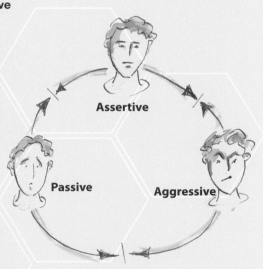

Behaviour where you back down in the face of someone else's demands or opinion and are left with a loss of self-esteem, or feeling as if you haven't expressed yourself fully, we call *passive* behaviour.

>>>

Aggressive behaviour is when you assert your wishes or opinion so strongly that you cross a line and leave another person feeling a loss of self-esteem or that they haven't been able to express themselves fully.

The definition of being assertive is 'having or showing a confident and forceful personality': you express your needs while allowing the other person to express theirs. As a leader, you need to learn to be assertive in a wide range of situations and, as your organisation grows, with a wide range of different types of people. Often the organisation leaders I speak to discover that as they get further out of their normal skill range as their company grows, they find themselves either backing down much more often than they would like, or getting exasperated and snappy with people out of the frustration of not knowing how to deal with new and complex issues.

It's important to recognise that your version of being aggressive may not take the form of shouting loudly or overtly losing your temper. Being sarcastic or cold with people are forms of aggression, often called passive-aggressive behaviour. Apply the test of whether you left the person feeling good about themselves, and you may quickly see that you use aggression more often than you think.

Passive behaviour often masquerades as 'being nice', 'being one of the gang' or 'being easy-going'. The test in this case is whether you end up feeling as if *you* always give in and never get what *you* need.

So let's assume that, like me, you think it would be a good idea to extend the range of situations and people where you can use assertive behaviour reliably and consistently most of the time. What steps do you need to take?

The first thing to explore is why you react differently in some situations from others. Why do you sometimes fail to stand up for yourself, and sometimes lose your cool, in apparently similar situations? You'll find more about the mechanism behind this in Chapter 9, but for the moment it's enough to say that any responses other than assertive ones usually come from some kind of fear.

If you tend to the easy-going, passive end of the spectrum as an organisational leader it's often from the fear of becoming unpopular, or being rejected by the people who used to be your peers and workmates. Or you may be afraid of rejection if you pick up the phone to certain prospects – if they sound busy or snappy, for example.

>>>

If your responses tend towards the aggressive, it's very often from a fear of loss of control – 'Why won't they do what I want?' – so you escalate your communication in the hope that you can force others through sheer force of personality. Explore your inner fears and motivations and start to challenge dysfunctional thoughts, and thereby behaviour, maybe with the help of a coach, until the unexpressed fear no longer runs the show.

Some hints

- The key word to use is: 'I'. In aggressive and passive modes, we tend to use the word 'you', which can sound like an attack, or hide behind the collective – 'We all think…' Instead, try 'I feel…', 'I believe…', 'I think…', 'In my opinion…'

- Don't say 'You should do this…' or 'You ought to do that…' – it can be interpreted as aggressive. Try saying 'I would like you to do this' or 'I feel it would be a good idea if you…'

- Don't state your opinion or perception as the truth. Rather state it as something you believe or feel. The other person will be much more likely to listen to you without getting defensive.

- If someone is doing something that upsets you, try using this four-part 'I' statement:
    - *When you…* (tell them what they do – the facts).
    - *I feel…* (tell them how you feel – your emotional reaction).
    - *Because…* (tell them why you feel like that – your fear, belief or perception).
    - *And I end up…* (tell them how you end up acting or behaving as a result).

    Then you can make a straight request as to what you would like them to do instead. See 'Working communication skill no. 8', p113, for more on making straight requests.

    For example: '*When you* ignore the security rules, *I feel* worried *because* I worry that I can't do my job properly, *and I end up* getting snappy with you. Please would you follow the procedures in future?'

- Body language is important. Sometimes your state of mind will show in your body language, even if you think you are controlling the words that come out of your mouth. Conduct a check when you want to be assertive: use normal eye contact and a relaxed, upright posture. Keep your voice even and normal and don't stand too close to the other person.

Chapter 7

You're their leader – but you're not there to tell them what to do

Working communication skill no. 7: learning to ask good questions

Chapter 7 – You're their leader – but you're not there to tell them what to do

- 'It's not my job to check on them – they are responsible for doing their bit.'
- 'I've got work to do; why don't they just get on with theirs?'
- 'I'm a leader now. People should treat me with respect.'
- 'It's like managing a bunch of kids. When are they going to show some responsibility [like me]?'

Before going into detail on some of the working communication skills that you will need to work with people who are, at least in the work context, not your friends, let's just do a mindset check.

The prevailing mindset

It would be easy at this stage, having got the concept of *not* trying to be people's friend at work, to flip completely to the opposite extreme and decide to become some kind of autocratic boss figure, based on your earliest assumptions of what a boss should be.

Callum did this.

Callum had for a long time been a successful sales representative with a large multinational company selling medical equipment. He had at one time wanted to be a doctor, and it was this commitment to helping people and saving lives that drove his passion for the company's products and his job selling them. Not surprisingly, he was very successful and created strong lasting relationships with his clients.

Which made it all the more startling when, promoted to regional sales manager, Callum adopted a style of leadership best described as remote. He spent hours working behind a closed door on paperwork, largely ignored his team, and only emerged when something went wrong, to deliver reprimands and orders. Within six months his very mature and experienced team was in uproar, demotivated and angry, and results had plummeted.

During coaching sessions we worked to explore why this gentle, committed and personable man had turned into Attila the Hun. We discovered together that this was his picture of what a manager should be, clearly based on his early experience in sales. However, although he understood this, Callum still struggled to find an alternative place to come from in managing his team. So, we explored the concept of partnership...

A more productive mindset

There's an old story about a man who, wanting to decide whether to go to heaven or hell when he died, decided to do some research. So he journeyed to the gates of hell and asked for a tour. When he entered he was confronted by an amazing scene: a table, groaning with delicious food and drink, looking absolutely wonderful. 'Well', he thought, 'this doesn't look bad. I could handle a few millennia here.' Then he saw that the people surrounding the table were thin and gaunt, clearly suffering from dreadful hunger and thirst, and he realised that though they had a spoon, the spoon was so long, and fastened to their hand in such a way, as to make it impossible for them to eat. So they were doomed for all time to be tortured by the sight and smell of a delicious banquet they were unable to enjoy.

'I don't want this', thought the man, and set off on his journey again. Arriving at the Pearly Gates, he requested a tour of heaven – and was greeted by exactly the same sight: the groaning table, the delicious scents and sights – and the people with exactly the same long spoons.

But what was the difference?

Well, I asked Callum that question, and after a short period of thought, he realised the answer: the people in heaven were feeding each other.

Partnership

This is the essence of partnership at work – you come to work with your focus on the others around you: how can *you* make *them* successful? How can you ensure that they deliver what's needed first time, with the minimum of fuss, conflict and hassle? Not because it will make *your* life easier (though it will) but because it's one of your values, the right thing to do. You're an essential part of the hive, just like everybody else, and if you do your bit right and work for the good of the whole, everyone will thrive.

And what effect did it have on Callum? Well, remember he already had outstanding working communication skills – with his clients, if not his team. With the new mindset in place, it was immediately obvious to him what he should do now. He went to all his team members individually, apologised for the way he had been behaving and booked time to go out with each of them for a day. He listened to their issues and needs and asked each of them what they needed in the way of support. He made promises, and he fulfilled them. Within weeks, the team were happy and motivated again, communicating well with Callum, and results were back on the up.

What are outstanding working communication skills?

Callum already had most of the working communication skills we are talking about and had been using them effectively for some years. He's a very good example of someone whose mindset had suddenly become skewed by an unexpected limiting belief, in this case about leadership and management, which temporarily made it impossible for him to use his normally excellent relationship-building and people skills. This limiting belief had cut in quite unexpectedly only when he was promoted quite late in his career – a hazard to watch for in your development as a leader.

The skills I'm talking about are the ones we've been exploring at the end of each chapter:

1. Negotiating and using an effective set of working *groundrules* – rules of engagement for working effectively together. In social relationships we usually let these emerge naturally, but in professional working relationships, where we are *paid* to work effectively with whatever people we meet, it makes sense to negotiate a clear set of groundrules at the outset, and to adjust these as our working relationships develop.
2. The skills of working *on* your business, not just *in* it.
3. Setting direction and agreeing *SMART* – specific and measurable – *objectives* for yourself and others.
4. *Managing your time effectively* and doing the right things first.
5. *Listening* effectively. Again, in social relationships, we learn to listen well enough for social purposes, to people we like and are naturally drawn to. There is a whole other level of skill needed to listen in all kinds of circumstances, to people with whom we may not feel a natural rapport, and to topics with which we may not agree.
6. Being *assertive* and controlling your reactions with different people and in challenging situations.
7. *Asking effective questions* that get to the nub of problems and enable people to find the right solutions.
8. Using direct communication: *making clear requests*, and learning to give, and get, one of three clear *responses* in return: a promise, a 'no', or a counter-offer. Keeping your promises.
9. Questioning your automatic judgements and *giving clear specific feedback* to individuals based on their behaviour, not on your perceptions of their personality.
10. *Meeting one-to-one* with people who work for and with you as a way of staying in touch with and motivating them.

The importance of your mindset

Having good communication skills is not enough on its own to ensure that people respond well to you, communication breakdowns won't happen and you become an effective leader. We've all encountered the person who has clearly just been on the latest training programme and is practising their newly learned skills on us. I'm thinking of the call centre operative who calls you and makes rather too much use of your name, while asking questions clearly designed to nudge you along a path that you just know will lead to a sales close at the end of the conversation. This person is not motivated by partnership or what's best for you. Test it by resisting or trying to say no, and see how quickly their false friendliness falls away. Trying to get someone to do what you want by practising your skills on them is at best clumsy and, at worst, manipulation of a truly unpleasant kind.

BELIEVE ME, GUYS, EVERYONE FROM THE CAPTAIN ON DOWN IS AN EQUALLY VALUED MEMBER OF THE TEAM

The thing that makes the difference in getting others on your side and sparking their enthusiasm and motivation is your *attitude* to them. Skills without an attitude of partnership and contribution are empty and manipulative, and however excellently you perform, others will see through you if you are not coming from what's best for them and the organisation you lead. It may take some self-examination to explore your own attitude and motivation towards leading others; are you motivated by ego and self-interest, or by a genuine wish to lead an organisation that thrives and in which people thrive too?

What does partnership mean for you?

This notion of partnership needs a little exploration. What most people think it means when they first encounter it is some version of 'I will if you will' – they will only give in a relationship if they first see proof that the other person is going to give too. And if there's a breakdown in communication, and one person feels they've been doing all the giving, then they feel entitled to withdraw their generosity, and cease to give until the other person makes some gesture of contrition and generosity, so that the giving can begin again. That's not true partnership.

Partnership is an attitude in the mind of an individual, and it's completely independent of whether anybody at all feels the same or behaves in the same way. Now, I'm not suggesting martyrdom here. You have no obligation to remain in a friendship, a working relationship – or indeed a marriage – if you consistently behave in the spirit of partnership and never get anything in return, but behaving this way doesn't *entitle* you to anything, and your choice of attitude doesn't have to be *dependent* on their behaviour. As a matter of fact, behaving in this way is very likely to elicit support and generosity on the part of others in the relationship, but if you are really behaving in the spirit of this mindset, you are not doing it in order to elicit any result at all. You are doing it because it is who you are, one of your core values.

If you're like many of us, here you might find a mean little voice in your head starts to whisper, 'But what's in it for me?' There may be nothing in it for you at all (though that's unlikely); it's a choice you make about how to behave towards the other people in your life and work. The reward you get, if any, is to feel good about how you behave towards others, knowing that you've treated them with dignity and respect, and as you would wish to be treated yourself.

Partnership at work

Can you imagine what it would be like working in a team, or a department, or a whole organisation, where this definition of partnership formed one of the core values, and where everybody (largely – they're all human, after all) behaved in accordance with these principles? You could come to work knowing that whatever you did, your colleagues would have your back – they'd be looking out for you and ensuring you were successful in your work. And they'd be doing this secure in the knowledge that they likewise were safe; no one would be waiting for them to make a mistake and finger pointing when they did. All of you would be looking to support each other and making sure everyone succeeded. It really is possible to have a workplace like this – if you as the leader have this as your vision and set up the hive so that that's the favoured behaviour.

Unfortunately, human hives aren't mostly set up this way – people are managed as individuals, with individual targets, and placed in competition with each other. But that's because, as we have seen, there's a knee-jerk assumption that organisations have to look like that. They don't, and you are free to set your expectations differently, supported by reward systems based not on the individual, but on teams working in partnership together. All you have to do is consciously to guide your organisation that way, involve your team in inventing creative ways to work together and reward themselves, and build reward and remuneration structures that support working in partnership, not against each other. It's your organisation, and you're its leader – what would you like it to look like?

How do you apply this mindset to your leadership?

- Focus on others and what you can do for them, ahead of what they can do for you. For most people, this is not an instinctive mindset, so you will need to make a conscious choice to do this.
- Trust that if you discipline yourself to stay in this mindset, relationships will work better, and ultimately you and your team or organisation will reap the rewards. It's counter-intuitive – but it works.
- Set targets and reward achievement at the team level as far as possible. Even in a system already based on the individual, with a bit of creativity you can add team targets and rewards – if you're committed to working this way.
- Train yourself to be supportive or generous not in order to get any specific outcome, but for its own sake. Role model this behaviour and insist that others behave this way too.
- Make it clear to your team that self-seeking behaviour will not be supported or rewarded. If any member of your team is struggling, be the first to offer support and help, and insist others do likewise.
- Failure of one member of the team is a *team* failure – teach team members to work for the success of *everyone* in the team.

I don't pretend we have all the answers. But the questions are certainly worth thinking about.

Arthur C. Clarke

One of the most important skills you can learn as a leader is to listen, which we have already covered (see 'Working communication skill no. 5', p61). One of the things we mentioned then is the fact that asking questions doesn't necessarily make you a good listener, because however good you are at asking questions, you are by definition coming from your own side of the track – you are thinking about what *you* need to know and what information *you'd* like to find out.

However, there are some ways of asking questions that are better than others. Most of us are familiar with the distinction between closed and open questions: closed questions result in a 'yes/no' answer or in a piece of specific information: 'What is your name?' is a closed question. These questions can be useful to slow someone down, or close a conversation, but they will kill an open-ended conversation or interview.

For many of us, our education has taught us to ask lots of closed questions. Experienced and educated leaders often feel that part of what they are there for is to know the answers and get to them as quickly as possible, and in seeking information or troubleshooting a problem it often seems that the quickest way to a solution is to drill down by asking closed questions.

However, in the area of engaging and motivating people, empowering them to find the answers themselves, or building truly durable solutions rather than quick fixes – all skills needed in developing and growing a healthy and sustainable organisation – it helps to have an alternative mode of questioning – and some questions are more open than others.

ALL THOSE IN FAVOUR SAY "YES"

Open questions

The usual guideline is that open questions begin with the words *when, where, how, why, what* and *who*, but it's not always quite as simple as that. As you can see from these examples, you can still ask closed questions using these words:

- 'When were you born?'
- 'Where were you when the accident happened?'
- 'How did you store the explosive?'
- 'Why were you in the kitchen yesterday evening?'
- 'What's your favourite colour?'
- 'Who is your role model?'

>>>

It often seems to me that I get results with people in direct correlation with the quality of the questions I ask them, and I sometimes spend a lot of time working out exactly the right way to pose a question to a client or group.

Detailed questions

Here are some wonderful questions for finding out more about people and what motivates them.

To find out about their goals and aspirations:

- 'How will you know when you have achieved that goal?'
- 'What will your life be like when you are able to…?'
- 'What will you see? Hear? Feel? (When the goal is achieved.)'
- 'How will you feel when the problem is solved?'

To examine current reality and their reality:

- 'What is happening now? What… Who… When… How often?'
- 'What did you make that mean?'
- 'Where does the problem lie, in the task or how you feel about it?'
- 'What rules or assumptions are you using that could be challenged?'
- 'What is the effect or result of that?'
- (In answer to 'I don't know'): 'I know you don't know, but if you did know?' (A weirdly effective question, this one.)

To help someone explore all their options:

- 'What do you think you could do in this situation?'
- 'How would you deal with this if you were (a guru, a hero, the best manager in…)?'
- 'What would you do if (your bonus, job, life, etc.) depended on your solving this issue?'
- 'What would you do now if you were already the person you know you have the potential of becoming?'
- 'What else could you do?'
- 'What would you do now if you knew you could not fail?'
- 'What if (this or that constraint) were removed?'

>>>

- 'What are the benefits and downsides of each option?'
- 'What factors will you use to weigh up the options?'

To establish their motivation and level of commitment:

- 'So what will you do next, and when?'
- 'Will this address your goal?'
- 'If you could have this right now, on a plate, would you take it?'
- 'How likely is this option to succeed?'
- 'What might stop you from achieving your goal?'
- 'What might it be useful to believe?'
- 'How will you overcome this?'
- 'What needs to happen for...?'
- 'What resources do you need to support you in this?'
- 'What's your first step? Second? Third?'
- 'On a scale of 1 to 10 how compelled are you to do this?'

Some hints

- When you've asked a good open question, leave a loooong silence. It will seem embarrassingly long to you, but the person you have asked the question of needs the time to think – and I promise you, the silence won't seem half as long to them as it will to you.

- Resist the temptation to follow up your initial question with more questions – they're still thinking about your first question. The urge to do this comes from embarrassment – hold your nerve.

- Start collecting good questions, and keep a list of the best. Until you are very skilled your mind will tend to go blank in the heat of a conversation or interview, and your instinct will be to fill the void with a quick (closed) question. Keep a list in your folder or tablet and have them discreetly in front of you.

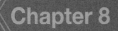

Chapter 8

What can we count on you for?

Working communication skill no. 8:
direct communication

Chapter 8 – What can we count on you for?

- 'Sorry I'm late – the phone rang.'
- 'I know I said I'd do it, but it's been manic this week.'
- 'Yes, you did say the deadline was the end of last month, but it's only been a week or so – what are you making a fuss about?'
- 'I was going to do it, but then they didn't do their bit, so I couldn't finish it.'

Do you hear these phrases around you? I do – all the time. It may just be me, but it seems that promises these days don't actually mean that someone will do what they said. It's more like an approximation – they'll work to your agreement, or your deadline, 'as long as'. As long as nothing comes up. As long as they don't fall ill. As long as they remember.

I don't want to make it sound as if I'm squeaky clean either – none of us is. In general, because I think about this particular mindset a lot, I'm a lot better than I used to be at doing what I said I'd do and turning up on time or hitting deadlines. But if I'm really honest, because I know this is the prevailing mindset, I sometimes use it. I know if I'm running late, I can always blame the traffic – because everyone does. I'm not proud of it, but I can get away with it, if I'm having a bad day.

The prevailing mindset

That's how it works, the prevailing mindset. Like all mindsets, it works because people collude with it. We all have bad days, when it's good to know that others will forgive you for running late or missing a deadline. So we collude, because we know that if we don't hold others to account too rigorously, then they'll let us off lightly when we slip on *our* agreements.

But at work, it's a nightmare:

Anita is a marketing and social media specialist. She runs internet-based marketing campaigns for her clients, which are very successful in helping them generate new leads and sales. Everything begins with the client's website, so the starting point of Anita's work is to conduct a thorough review of their website, if necessary rebuilding it so that the new marketing campaign will direct customers to carefully tailored landing pages and attractively branded graphics and information. Because Anita is not a specialist herself, she works with freelance web designers to do this part of the work.

Anita prides herself on making and keeping to unambiguous agreements with her clients, and always explains this clearly when she starts to work with a new website designer. But she's tearing her hair out trying to work out how she can get across to her suppliers that she really means what she says.

Anita came to me a few months ago for help in negotiating a new agreement with a young woman whose work she really rated, but who didn't seem able to keep to the deadlines clearly agreed at the outset of each project. I have to admit, when I started this small project, I assumed that Anita couldn't be making herself as clear as she thought she was, but I was astonished to find that the young designer, Kirsty, definitely remembered and understood the conversations about deadlines. She just didn't think they mattered, and was actually quite angry and upset with Anita for 'putting me under pressure'. In the end, Anita reluctantly had to accept that Kirsty simply didn't want to comply with what she thought were unreasonable expectations. So Kirsty lost the work, and Anita lost a talented and creative member of her team – a lose–lose result, especially as Kirsty still thinks Anita was being unfair.

A more productive mindset

The story above reflects a widespread attitude to accountability in our culture – not only that it's hard to make and keep promises, but that it might even be impossible and, in any case, that it's stressful, unreasonable and unfair to set such standards for ourselves, let alone others.

But the story also demonstrates that it's stressful and unproductive not to be able to count on others and ourselves at work and in our personal lives. In fact, my experience of learning this lesson in life has been that I spend much less time and experience much less stress just by making clear promises and keeping them. It's much less effort than resisting, wriggling, thinking up excuses and worrying about other people's reactions to my missing the deadline.

The first step in taking accountability is to *choose* to be accountable for an outcome. This is regardless of whether you know how to achieve it, or believe you can do it. Gandhi did not know how to achieve independence for India when he assumed leadership for the movement. And there were many times when he doubted his own ability. But he chose to be accountable for the outcome, spoke out and continued to stand for his vision in the face of all the circumstances.

And it *is* a choice. There are many things we would *like* to achieve, or to have happen in the world. But we do not *choose* to be accountable for everything – accountability starts with the choice.

The term 'accountability', far from being the loose concept that the prevailing mindset would suggest, is actually an interaction between your attitude to being held to account, and your relationship with the circumstances that might get in the way. You could think of it as operating at three levels as shown in Table 5.

Table 5 – What level of accountability do you mostly operate at?

State of accountability	Relationship with the task	Relationship with the circumstances
3. Proactive	Willing to be held to account	• Not necessarily a barrier to delivery • Seek to understand them • Work creatively to go beyond them • Will even create favourable circumstances to get a result
2. Conditional	Willing to be held to account (subject to circumstances)	• Good excuse when things go wrong • Avoid dealing effectively with them
1. Resistant	Resists and avoids being held to account (because of the circumstances)	• Resigned about them • Use them as an excuse for not trying

At level 1, you might resist and avoid being held to account. You can't do it, in your mind, 'because…' Because you're too busy. Because the traffic is so unreliable. Because someone else lets you down. You're a helpless victim of the circumstances (in your mind) and they become your excuse for not trying. There'll be some aspect of your life or work that feels to you like this. If you think there isn't, it's probably because the impossibility of overcoming this particular set of circumstances is so real for you that it doesn't even feel to you like a mindset. It's just the way things are. At this level we avoid being accountable or hide behind the circumstances. All of us do this in some area of our life or work, but somebody who is being fully accountable will be honest about whether they have made a conscious choice to do so or are just being a victim.

At level 2, you *feel* you're being much more accountable. You're ready and willing to be held to account, 'as long as'. As long as the traffic isn't too bad. As long as the market holds up. As long as 'they' don't let you down. But can you see that you are just as much a victim of the circumstances here? Everything depends on something outside yourself – and the really insidious thing is that you'll be able to get lots of people to agree with you that those circumstances really might get in your way. Most people would buy in to the busyness of everyday life, the awfulness of the traffic or the unreliability of other people. You've got a ready-made excuse all lined up for when you fail – and anyone would sympathise, wouldn't they? People at this level are difficult, if not impossible, to manage. A fully accountable person will never believe the *reason* for failing to deliver on a commitment is an *excuse* for doing so.

So how much more accountable could you be? Well, you could be the kind of person who at level 3 recognises that circumstances exist and factors them in. They make promises *allowing* for the traffic, the unexpected interruption, the unreliable supplier. And on top of that, they work all the time to make sure that the circumstances as far as possible don't go wrong. They set out early (earlier

OK, I ADMIT IT, WE'RE LOST, BUT THE IMPORTANT THING TO DO IS REMAIN FOCUSED ON WHOSE FAULT IT IS

than most people would think necessary). They bar the phone and lock their door, and say no to new commitments until they've completed what they've promised. And they've learned to chase their suppliers, *before* giving them a chance to fail.

And do they always succeed? Well, no, they don't – sometimes the circumstances are just too intractable – but they always try. Their attitude to tricky circumstances is, 'bring them on', and they work tirelessly to anticipate what might go wrong. And if they fail at the end of all that – they take it on the chin. They don't make excuses or blame the circumstances or other people. They just say, 'I failed. I apologise.' Then they learn what they can from the failure and move on. People operating at this level are a pleasure to manage and to have as team colleagues.

Managing people at the different levels of accountability

Actually, it's not that hard to manage people at level 1 – their resistance is usually pretty clear. The key is nearly always to challenge their relationship with the circumstances.

One of the memorable breakthroughs I had with a client group was with a very senior director, a member of a board that always met at one of the airport hotels at Heathrow, to the west of London. He was always late, and always had what sounded like a plausible excuse, usually to do with the traffic, which indeed is usually very bad. This might have worked with a lesser group, but he was trying to use this excuse with a group of about eight equally busy people, all of whom always managed to be there on time!

We all struggled to get him to understand that in our view, it wasn't too much to ask that he should be at the meetings on time. Eventually, I asked him, 'Peter, do you ever go on holiday?' He looked at me as if I was mad. 'Of course', he said. 'Well', I said. 'Do you ever travel from Heathrow Airport?' 'Yeees', he replied, beginning to suspect where I was going with this line of questioning. 'Well, how often have you ever missed the plane?' He went silent as he reflected on the implications of the question. He was only late, it seemed, when it was 'only' his colleagues waiting for him. He assumed they would collude with his excuses and not call him on his tendency to keep them all waiting. But when it came to possibly missing the plane to go on holiday, there was nothing he wouldn't do to make sure he was there in good time.

It was all he needed to finally get his act together, and he was never again late for a board meeting.

Managing people operating at level 3 is, as you can imagine, a joy. Just make sure the agreement is clear, and step out of their way. In fact, it can be quite a shock managing someone who operates at this level, because they spend so little time cooking up excuses for why it can't be done, or can't be done on time, that they seem to get on with things faster than you would have thought possible. My business partner and I have a highly respected member of our support team, who never makes a fuss and never misses a deadline. In fact, we've learned not to email her in the evenings or at weekends to suggest an idea we've just had, because we've learned that she usually just does it. Right there and then. She knows that it's often quicker to do it (within reason) than to waste time adding it to a list or wondering where she's going to find the time. But we are not used to people operating that way, so we are embarrassed to find she's given up a small part of her private time to do something for us.

The real problem is managing people at level 2. They look willing – in fact, if you ask them to do something, they pretty much always say yes (sound familiar?). But, as in the story about Kirsty above, there's always some reason why it didn't happen. In fact, what's going on here is also resistance, but the person has learned that it's not a good idea to look too resistant in work situations. So they seem keen and willing, but you can't count on them. If you suggest that they work on the circumstances, such as for example calling someone they are relying on to make sure that *they* don't miss *their* deadline, they will usually say, 'But I shouldn't have to', or 'But I've got enough to do, doing my own job. Do I have to do theirs as well?'

What they haven't understood is that, in making a promise and accepting a standard and a deadline for a piece of work, they have made it their job to manage *every aspect* of the process it takes to fulfil that promise. This is an attitude change that can take some intensive coaching to shift. One thing that often works is to point out that they could refuse to take the job on. A clear 'no' is much easier to manage than a 'maybe'. Most people don't want to take the consequences of saying 'no', so this then forces them to consider how they might be able to say 'yes' and still ensure that they are able to deliver. See the 'Working communication skill' section at the end of this chapter for some guidelines on direct communication.

- Approach with caution. Work on *yourself* first, and be scrupulously honest about whether or not you're behaving at an appropriate level of accountability. Make sure you are squeaky clean – your management and coaching of others will only be effective if it's based on your own experience. *No one* is above behaving at level 1.
- Equally, nobody operates at level 3 accountability all the time. Don't kid yourself – and sort yourself out.
- If you really can't see yourself doing something, say 'no'. Of course you'll also have to deal with the reaction, but it's much easier for the other person to deal with a 'no' than a conditional 'yes'. It also has the merit of being honest, and of not leaving you with the guilt and worry of a task that you know in your heart won't be done properly or on time.
- Manage people's expectations – if you let people know you're going to be late *before* you actually are late, and in good time for them to react, you are at least still being accountable. You still need to be aware that they may not be very happy with you though.
- Be mindful/aware of what's going on in your head when you make a promise – don't make one if there is, at the time of making it, *any* foreseeable chance of breaking it. Or factor in right at the outset the time and extra effort it will take to fulfil the promise.
- In working with others, always insist on a clear 'no' or a clear 'yes'. You'll see if they are wriggling.
- Recognise also that you may have to manage the process to ensure they don't let you down. It's not doing their job for them; it's part of the job of managing people to be successful. Don't do it for ever, but be willing to train people for a reasonable period when you are beginning to work this way.
- There's a lot of collusion with conditional accountability out there. Recognise this and create explicit agreements with your team members that 'we don't do it that way here'. They'll be surprised, but when they get it, they'll be grateful.

If you have an important point to make, don't try to be subtle or clever. Use a pile driver. Hit the point once. Then come back and hit it again. Then hit it a third time – a tremendous whack.

Winston Churchill

A very straightforward and simple skill this one, yet one that many people, especially in certain cultures and countries, seem to have missed learning or actively avoid: the skill of making a simple, direct *request*, and giving, in return, a simple unequivocal *response*.

What does a request sound like?

Person A says something like, 'Please do X (task) by Y (date).'

Easy, you may think. What could go wrong with that? Well in the UK, where I live and work, we are often brought up to think it rude to make direct requests, so we spend a lot of time fudging and padding: 'Do you think you could just…', 'Would you mind awfully…', 'Shall we try to…' etc. Or we drop hints: 'It would be great if somebody would…' or get sarcastic: 'Is anybody ever going to…? Eventually we may even crack and have a tantrum: 'I've had it. Doesn't anybody ever do anything around here?'

Some cultures of course would just laugh at this. Most Dutch people, or Germans or US citizens have very little trouble making straight requests, and think we in the UK are ridiculously woolly about such things. But even they have trouble with the responses…

What does a response sound like?

There are only three clear direct responses to a straight request:

Person B may make a *promise*:	'Yes' – full accountability. They'll get it done whatever the circumstances, and if they fail, they'll take the consequences on the chin.

>>>

They may *decline* the request:	'No' – they honestly don't see themselves doing it, and are willing to take the consequences of saying 'no' to you.
Or they may make a *counter-offer*:	'I won't do X by Y, but I will do it by Z'. They think carefully about whether they can do it and under what circumstances and make a proposal to you.

If you first discipline yourself to make clear, direct requests and responses like this, and then train everyone around you to do likewise, it will make a bigger difference to your business than you could ever imagine.

Some hints

- You don't just need to make well-formed requests, but also to manage the responses, especially at first. Many people will be vague and not make a clear promise, decline or counter-offer, and even if they apparently do, they may forget or let it slide.

- You will want to resist managing their response too – why should you do their job for them? Well, because you are a leader, training others in a new, more effective working skill. They won't get it right straight away and will need coaching and hands-on management for a while.

- There is a danger for everyone at first of over-promising – train yourself and others around you to check their diaries and make realistic promises, rather than just always saying 'yes'.

- If you say 'no', someone might not like it. You have to be willing to take the consequences of this (fear of this is one reason we fudge).

- As a leader, be prepared to accept a 'no' sometimes too – your response to this is critical in training others to give honest responses.

- Learning to make good counter-offers is the key: 'I can't talk now, but come back at 3pm and I'll be able to give you my full attention', 'It's missed the post today, but I'll send it special delivery tomorrow' or 'I can't fit this in to my current workload, but if it's more important than X task, I could prioritise it. Which would you prefer me to complete first?'

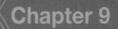

Chapter 9

The voice in your head

Working communication skill no. 9:
tackling negative thoughts and limiting beliefs

Chapter 9 – The voice in your head

- 'I'm sure everybody feels more confident than me.'
- 'They all think I'm great – if they only knew how useless I really am.'
- 'I'm the only one around here who knows what they are doing – why can't they all be more like me?'
- 'Those idiots over in (marketing, HR, accounts, production – fill in the gap) – why can't they just do their jobs properly?'
- 'Don't ask me to make the presentation – I'd die.'

Do you have a little voice in your head? If you think you don't, tune in again: it's the little voice saying, 'What on earth is she talking about? I don't have a little voice.' It's the one that says, 'Oh no, is it that time already?' when the alarm goes off in the morning. We all have one – it's what the psychologists call your 'internal dialogue', and it's been with human beings ever since we had language to express ourselves. It's like a parrot, sitting on your shoulder and whispering in your ear. Tune in, and you'll realise that it's there all the time.

The prevailing mindset

Most people think that the running commentary that goes on in their head is who they are – the sum total of all those thoughts, opinions, fears, joys and emotional reactions that in some way makes them, them. You hear people say things like:

- 'I can't help how I am.'
- 'I just say it as I see it.'
- 'I'm very (shy, nervous, decisive, nice, nasty – fill in the gap...).'
- 'What can you do? He's just like that.'
- 'You can't change who you are.'

...all of which doesn't give you very much scope to change, grow, or improve your own or anyone else's behaviour.

Indeed, sometimes when I introduce this idea to people, they will accuse me of trying to change their personality, so closely do they identify with every last thought they ever have.

It's not always a problem, of course. The parrot is often what keeps you safe in life – think of the one that says, 'Slow down, you're going too fast', on the road, or 'Let's get out of here', when a dispute kicks off in a bar. That is of course how it originated – an articulation of early man's instincts, as he learned what was safe in life and what wasn't and then learned to put words to it.

However, because it originated as part of an instinct to keep us safe, it's not always saying nice warm friendly things (if you're saying warm, encouraging and nurturing things to yourself, don't change a thing). But listen to yourself in a situation where you feel uncomfortable, and the voice will be suspicious and defensive: 'What did she mean by that?' 'Who does he think he is?' 'Did I make a fool of myself?' 'I'm not taking that from her.'

In working life, our self-limiting beliefs affect whether we are successful and the organisation we work in is a satisfying place to be. Here are some common self-limiting beliefs:

- 'You can't trust anybody.'
- 'Hard work is noble.'
- 'Fulfilling work is for others, not me.'
- 'Fulfilment comes from my personal life, not my work life.'
- 'I'm too old to make major changes to the way I work.'
- 'My family and friends will think I'm crazy.'
- 'I'm a fraud – my success is a result of the corporate structure.'
- 'The unknown isn't safe.'
- 'I'm afraid of failing.'
- 'It's a dog-eat-dog world.'

People are very different in how their voice evolves. Some of us turn it in on ourselves, some point the finger at others – and some of us do a bit of both, depending on how strong and on top of things we feel. The examples I give aren't necessarily all from the same person, though it's possible for one person's parrot to be very inconsistent. Some are confident, almost arrogant, and others are scared and unconfident. Clients sometimes say they have two parrots, arguing with each other, and some confess to having a whole flock!

A more productive mindset

It's easy to blame external circumstances when you get stopped short in life – your manager, lack of time, a change in the market... But if anything really stops you, it's likely to be a thought about yourself, reinforced by emotion: a self-limiting belief. An event occurred. You drew a conclusion about it and absorbed it emotionally. Figure 7 shows how the process works.

Figure 7 – How limiting beliefs begin

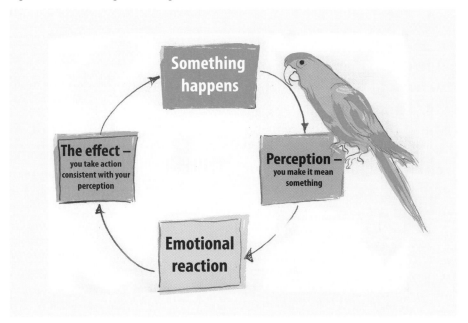

We all have our own rich personal history of events – from parents, educators, our culture, gender and work experience – and, as a result, we've developed our own unique perspectives on the world and ourselves.

Your beliefs stay with you for three primary reasons. First, you *label* them. ('I'm no good at business finance. Nobody in my family can do maths.') Labelling beliefs and focusing on where they come from helps you to rationalise them and make them OK.

Then you engage in *selective data gathering*. You seek out evidence to support your beliefs and ignore evidence that would support the opposite belief. ('I made a mess of the budget presentation – everyone else was so confident.')

Finally, you disguise them – *sugar-coat them* – to make them more palatable. They become an ego advantage. For example, 'I'm not good at finance…' can become 'I'm just the creative type' – a more empowering belief (for you) which could aid, but is actually more likely to limit, your career.

Before long, you're on autopilot, with these now-subconscious beliefs guiding your actions in life. Many of these beliefs help sustain you, but others don't – they limit your ability to lead a happy and fulfilling life.

Here's the thing: that voice in your head isn't 'you', and you don't always have to do what it seems to be telling you to do. Listen to it by all means, but learn to make a conscious decision to act on it or not. There is a 'you' that can learn to stand back far enough to listen to the competing voices and make a considered decision as to which to listen to.

How do we know this? You may say, 'How can it not be me? They're in my head, they're my thoughts – aren't they?' Yes, of course they are, but you can teach yourself that your thoughts are not always wise or right. You do actually know this: if you've ever hauled yourself out of a warm comfy bed to go for a run, or turned down the doughnuts in favour of the fruit salad, you overrode your parrot. If you've ever got so frustrated with someone that you wanted to scream at them, or shake them, but didn't, you overrode your parrot. Your parrot almost certainly wanted the bed, or the sugar fix or to bop them on the nose – but you overrode it, didn't you?

This is probably the single greatest mindset shift in becoming a more effective leader or indeed a wiser human being: recognising that there is a 'you' that can listen to the endless soundtrack and choose whether to act on it or not. Unfortunately, some people never discover this – they eat themselves to death, get into fights in pubs, teach themselves to avoid situations that make them uncomfortable – all because they believe that the parrot voice is real, and that they must act on what it says. *Only some of it is useful*.

If you are willing to allow that this way of looking at how you think might be valid, and even useful, it gives you access to communicating more effectively in all kinds of situations.

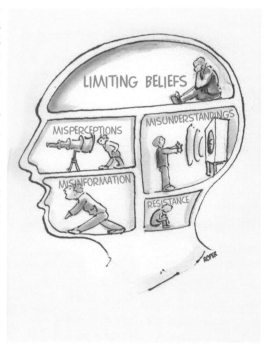

You're in a given situation, let's say at work. Something happens, or somebody says something. Your parrot says something about it (it always does). It's instantaneous and you may not even be aware of it, but it does say *something*. If what it says is positive and empowering, we can forget about it – no need to do anything. The emotional reaction will be positive and empowering too, and your actions will be natural and appropriate.

Your boss: 'Please would you have this report on my desk by the end of today?'
You (your parrot): 'Great. A meaty bit of work to get my teeth into this afternoon.'
Emotional reaction: Excitement, enthusiasm.
The effect: You get stuck in and do an excellent piece of work.

But let's say it's not so positive and empowering. Then your emotional reaction will equally be negative and disempowering.

Your boss: 'Please would you have this report on my desk by the end of today?'
You (your parrot): 'Oh, no. I hate reports. And that's far too short a time scale to make a good job of it.'
Emotional reaction: Annoyance, panic, anxiety.
The effect: You have a horrible afternoon, get a headache and are snappy and irritable with your colleagues.

And round we go again…

The effect of this process is even worse than just the effect on you: in the second scenario, what do you think the effect is on your work colleagues and your boss of your panicky and irritable mood? Only you can predict how they will react – but they *will* react to the atmosphere you create. And the possibility is that their reaction (Reciprocal irritation? Avoidance?) will make your mood worse.

Because this is how the process works. Others have parrots too – which in this case are saying something like, 'What's wrong with her?' and causing an emotional reaction in them. If they become irritable in return (a very common reaction), this may trigger even more irritability in you, neatly confirming their first impression. Before you know where you both are, you are stuck in a loop where they think you're irritable, so treat you abruptly. You dislike their treatment of you, so respond tersely, and each of you neatly proves your point about the other.

That's exactly how it works – and somebody has to be self-aware enough to break out of the cycle. This is where identifying that your parrot isn't always the right or the only way to react comes in handy. Maybe your colleague, instead of returning your irritation with a knee-jerk snappy response, might think to himself, 'That's a strange response. I wonder if she's feeling under pressure?' and come back to you with a concerned query, 'Are you OK? Is there anything I can do to help?' Hopefully (it doesn't always happen) this will trigger a different response in you, and your relationship is cemented rather than damaged.

An example:

Many years ago, as a lecturer in a further education college, I had a student, Sonia, who struck me as unusually slow on the uptake. If I asked the class to do a particular exercise, she did a different one. I'd tell them to read a certain page of their textbook, and discover that she had read the wrong page. Or I'd tell the whole class to go to a different classroom for their next lesson, and Sonia would turn up at the usual classroom.

I'm not at all proud of it, but as a busy teacher, what conclusion do you think my parrot came to? Yes, that's right. I (it) concluded that Sonia was a bit dim. And the really insidious thing about how this whole process operates is that, as teachers do, I started to share the episodes and anecdotes with my colleagues in the staffroom. Before long we had a mutual story going, that Sonia was the class dunce and, in fact, probably wouldn't make the grade on the course.

Suddenly one day, one of my colleagues came running into the staffroom. 'Guess what', she said. 'I just went up behind Sonia to ask her something, and she didn't respond at all. When I finally attracted her attention, I realised: she's deaf. All this time she's been trying to get away with leaving off her hearing aid, and lip-reading.'

Appalled, we replayed the incidents and realised that every one of them could be explained by the fact that Sonia, trying not to draw attention to herself, had not been in a position to see our lips as we spoke carelessly and too quickly for her. She wasn't unintelligent at all – and as we rewound, and talked to her, and started over again, she quickly became a confident and successful student, graduating two years later with distinction.

And the really shocking thing was the reason Sonia hadn't felt she could wear her hearing aid in the first place: she knew the assumptions that people would make about her when they first met her wearing one (people's parrots are full of prejudice). With the opportunity to make a fresh start at college and meet a new set of friends, she had made the decision to try to manage without from the start.

A flock of parrots makes a culture

This is one of the mechanisms you as an organisational leader will need to learn to manage and control. Notice how quickly the *story* about Sonia turned into the *truth* about Sonia in my working group. This is how office gossip gains currency and turns into 'the truth' about 'how it works around here'. Working with groups, I only have to ask, 'What do you (your parrot) *really* think about (that department over there, head office, your clients...)?' and, in the safe space of the training room, out it all comes: the myths, the beliefs, the decision the group made about somebody years ago...

Often, groups are shocked when they see the stories they have created, and even more so when we explore how these stories have affected their behaviour over the years.

Blocks and barriers

By holding these beliefs you limit what is possible in your own performance. At work, and especially if you are in a senior position, you ultimately limit what the organisation is capable of achieving. If you manage other people, you may tend to buy into their self-limiting beliefs. Where you are in the grip of a disempowering belief about yourself, you are unlikely to be the kind of coach who will inspire others to go beyond their own limitations.

Once you start to explore the impact of those initial perceptions on your own behaviour (and I would *strongly* recommend you explore the impact on *you* first, before beginning to use the concept in coaching and managing others), you'll realise that they can give rise to unexpected and only dimly understood blocks to your performance. For every situation where you find it impossible to be assertive, you are in the grip of a perception or belief that comes from your parrot. It's as if you're nailed in place by the foot, paralysed by the thought you have about the situation, and are incapable of moving or behaving naturally and appropriately.

In coaching clients, I very often find that the key to helping them to become more effective is *not* to train them in a new skill, but to help them uncover the belief, perception or attitude that is getting in their way – to take the nail out of their foot so they can move freely again. Sometimes they are startled when they discover what the parrot is saying to them – and shocked at the grip it has had on them. These unexamined beliefs and assumptions can have a surprisingly debilitating effect on us, and challenging and shedding them is amazingly freeing.

But aren't we stuck with our beliefs?

Beliefs can be changed. While they feel very real to the believer, they are not absolute – they are *learned*. When you have a genuine willingness to replace a belief with something new and empowering, it is entirely possible to do just that.

Throughout your lifetime, your beliefs change continually. Beliefs that you once thought to be immutable cease to be true. Take the example of Roger Bannister who, in 1957, became the first athlete to break the four-minute barrier for running a mile. Before this, it was conventional wisdom that a sub-four-minute mile was impossible. But that same year, 16 other athletes also ran a mile in less than four minutes. They didn't become superhuman overnight – as a direct result of Bannister's breakthrough run, their beliefs changed.

Like those milers, business people have their own unique sets of beliefs, some of which limit their potential. For instance, during a recession, the members of a sales force may all believe that strong sales are impossible. But if just one person increases their sales, what seemed an inevitable fact will suddenly appear more like a thin excuse for poor performance.

Here are some famous limiting beliefs from the past:

- 'I think there's a world market for maybe five computers' (Thomas Watson, chairman of IBM, 1943).
- 'There is no reason why anyone would want to have a computer in their home' (Ken Olson, president, chairman and founder of Digital Equipment Corp, 1977).
- 'This "telephone" has too many shortcomings to be seriously considered as a means of communication. The device is inherently of no value to us' (Western Union memo, 1876).
- 'Who the hell wants to hear actors talk?' (HM Warner, Warner Bros, 1927).
- 'We don't like their sound, and guitar music is on the way out' (Decca Recording Company rejecting the Beatles, 1962).
- 'Heavier than air flying machines are impossible' (Lord Kelvin, president, Royal Society, 1895).

…and finally…

- 'Everything that can be invented has been invented' (Charles H. Duell, commissioner, US Office of Patents, 1899).

Imagine what kind of world we'd be living in now if anybody had listened to *them*.

Create a can-do culture

The organisation that can overcome self-limiting beliefs in the minds of its workforce – including its leaders – will be the organisation that wins. This is why, in organisation development work, I start by looking in depth at the fundamental beliefs and values of the organisation's leaders.

You need to create an organisation culture in which the 'can do – will do' mentality thrives and becomes the norm. In this type of culture, success and achievement are expected and much more likely to happen – and you can only create a culture like this if you have tackled and conquered your own personal self-limiting beliefs.

How do you apply this mindset to your leadership?

- Work on yourself first. You need to have a clear understanding of how this psychological process operates and the humility to comprehend its grip on you, before you will have sufficient compassion to work on someone else. Other people's blocks often sound ridiculous to us.
- Use 'Working communication skill no. 9', p126 to unpick those situations where you know you are in the grip of a limiting belief or perception – use a trained coach if you find it too difficult to unstick yourself.
- When coaching someone else, the key is very often to explore the limiting belief, rather than to train them in new skills.
- We too quickly assume the need is for more training. If you give someone training on top of a limiting belief, you'll just waste the time and money you spend on the training.

People are always blaming their circumstances for what they are. I don't believe in circumstances. The people who get on in this world are the people who get up and look for the circumstances they want, and if they can't find them, make them.

George Bernard Shaw

Once you have become aware of your inner dialogue – the parrot on your shoulder – you'll start to notice it all the time. Sometimes, it says positive things to you: 'Looking good today', 'I made a good job of that', and so on. But very often it says negative things and affects your behaviour and your mood without your being consciously aware of the process. Often, the first thing you will notice is that you feel indefinably unconfident, or fearful or angry, without knowing why, or when the feeling started. We all have different reactions to the different triggers in our lives, so the first thing to do is to notice that you are in a negative mood or state, and *name* the emotion. There are four main categories your emotional state could fall into, and you can remember them by this simplified mnemonic: *mad, bad, glad or scared*. You may have your own choice of words for these emotions:

Mad: Might be 'angry', 'irritated', 'livid', 'annoyed', and so on.

Bad: Might be 'depressed', 'down', 'guilty', 'ashamed', 'embarrassed', and so on.

Glad: Could be 'happy', 'joyful', 'elated', 'proud'...

Scared: Could be 'terrified', 'anxious', 'worried', 'unsettled', and so on.

Find your own words for the emotion you are feeling, then:

1. Identify the situation.

   Describe the situation that triggered your negative mood. When did it start? What happened? What else was happening at the time? Be as specific as possible.

2. Identify automatic thoughts – your parrot.

   Make a list of all the automatic thoughts you had in response to the situation. This is the parrot on your shoulder, your inner dialogue, coming up with perceptions and trying to find meaning in the situation to explain your emotional reaction. Try to catch your own mind talking – what's it saying?

Some of us blame others: 'They're out to get me', 'He's a bully', as a first reaction, but underlying this will always be an opinion about yourself – that's what disempowers you. So we might say, 'He's a bully', but most of us wouldn't stop there and shrug it off – if we did, there would be no problem. We go on to beat ourselves up: 'Why can't I come up with a quick response?', 'What's wrong with me, that I feel so shaky when he starts in on me?', 'Why am I such a coward?', 'I'm useless', 'That's typical of me', 'I'm such an idiot', 'I always mess things up'.

3. Analyse your mood in detail – your emotional response.

Describe how you felt in the situation and how you're feeling now. Examples might include: angry, upset, frustrated, scared, anxious, depressed, betrayed, disgusted or embarrassed.

4. Describe the action you took.

Describe how a combination of your parrot and your emotions caused you to act in the situation: 'I felt shaky and walked away', 'I got defensive and shouted at her'.

Now go back and challenge the conclusions you came to.

5. Find objective supportive evidence.

Write down any evidence you can find that supports the automatic thoughts you listed in step 2. For 'I'm an idiot', you might write down, 'I messed up the presentation', and 'I missed the deadline and let the team down.' Come up with any and all thoughts you are having about the situation.

6. Find objective contradictory evidence.

Now look rationally at your automatic thoughts and write down objective evidence that contradicts the thought. Consider other people's perspectives as well – ask them, if necessary. Write down your new perspective. You might list successes you have had, good feedback you've received and people who respect and like you.

7. Identify fair and balanced thoughts.

Look again at the thoughts you wrote down in steps 5 and 6. Take a balanced view of the situation and write down your conclusions. So: 'OK, I messed up this presentation, but I've learned a lot, and I know how to do it next time. I've never done it before, and in fact I've had compliments on my presentations in the past. My colleagues respect me, and some of them have made mistakes too. I just feel sympathy; I never decide they are idiots.'

>>>

8. Monitor your present mood.

Take a moment to assess how you are feeling now. Do you feel better about the situation? Is there any action you need to take? Note any steps you need to take to feel better, to resolve the situation or maybe to put measures in place to make sure it never happens again.

Once you have done all this and taken time to digest this new way of looking at the situation, you will be able to think clearly, and make informed and sensible choices about what to do about it. One of the things you might choose to do is to give someone some feedback...

Giving feedback

You can use the parrot concept to produce well-formed pieces of feedback. Simply make sure that you include the first four steps in the cycle (the remaining steps above are for you to do in private, to unstick yourself and free up your ability to handle the situation better).

For example (positive feedback):

- Thank you. I particularly liked the way you dealt with the awkward questions from the supplier. (What happened/the facts.)
- I thought you sounded knowledgeable and confident. (Interpretation/ perception.)
- I was very pleased and impressed. (Emotional reaction.)
- I was able to make my points in the meeting and sound good too. (Action/ effect.)

Or (negative feedback):

- In our meeting, you kept passing all the questions the buyer asked to me. (What happened/the facts.)
- I felt it made me look unprepared and stupid. (Interpretation/perception.)
- And I got angry and upset with you. (Emotional reaction.)
- So I got flustered and couldn't answer them sensibly. (Action/effect.)

>>>

Some hints

- When describing what happened, be careful to choose objective, descriptive language and stick only to observable fact. Take care not to let your opinions or perceptions leak in to how you describe the situation.

- When describing your perceptions, use the word 'I' – 'I felt it made me look stupid', not 'You made me look stupid'. This is crucial – you are *owning* your perceptions and not accusing the other person of any intent.

- Again, *describe* your emotion as an observer might. Not 'You made me angry' but 'I became angry.'

- Stick to describing *your* perceptions and reactions. Don't try to describe theirs.

- It can help if you start to think of your automatic thoughts – your parrot – as in some ways independent of you. After all, you are able to listen to and describe them, aren't you? With practice, you can learn to identify more with this quiet inner observer than with the passing knee-jerk thoughts you have. And when you get into the habit of challenging your own perceptions for long enough, you'll realise that they are very often not as true as you might initially have thought.

Chapter 10

What's your leadership style?

Working communication skill no. 10:
holding one-to-one meetings with your direct
reports

Chapter 10 – What's your leadership style?

- 'My boss leaves me to get on with it – I love the independence.'
- '*My* boss leaves me to get on with it – I'm all at sea, and could do with some guidance.'
- 'As a leader, I believe in getting my sleeves rolled up and leading from the front.'
- 'I can't be bothered with holding my people's hands – I'm not here to do their job for them.'
- 'I like to feel we all do the work together as equals.'

Interesting, isn't it? There seem to be lots of contradictory ways of looking at how to lead and manage people, and as many ways of doing it as there are leaders and people to be managed.

The prevailing mindset

I've noticed that senior leaders tend to have a clear philosophy of how they like to manage people and how they'd like to be viewed by their team members. When asked, they tend to feel that a hands-on, command and control style is rather old-fashioned and that delegation and empowerment are desirable (and fashionable) styles of leadership to aim at.

That's in theory anyway. In practice, I generally find the majority of leaders I meet are quite controlling. They may *believe* in empowerment and delegation and will tell me that these are their chosen styles of leadership, but when I talk to their employees, their usual complaint is that they are micro-managed to within an inch of their lives and would love to have the freedom and space to get on with their jobs without interference.

Of course, the opposite can be true too: I do meet leaders who believe they are on top of the job and managing their team members rigorously and regularly. These team members, however, will often say they don't see enough of their team leader, or only see them when something has gone wrong and a crisis needs managing or someone needs to be disciplined.

The prevailing mindset among both the leaders and the led seems to be that there's a right style of leadership. From their reading of books and the media, people have absorbed a sense that there has been a movement away from a Victorian, command and control style towards a more egalitarian, even laissez-faire style of leadership, and if you ask them their philosophy of leadership, they will tell you that this is how proper leaders aspire to lead. But human nature seems to reassert itself, and organisation leaders generally find it very hard to leave alone the people who work for them, so in practice, they are actually much more hands-on than they think they are.

And those being led? Most adults in work dislike being treated, as they see it, like children, and once they know the job, resist too much interference, sometimes to the point where they will withhold management information from their leader, because they see his requesting it as interfering.

There's a mismatch, which can lead to nobody really getting what they need. Without understanding the mechanism governing this area of work, leaders end up feeling they either have no information, or they have to do their employees' jobs for them. Employees end up feeling crowded and mistrusted, or, should they succeed in getting their leader to back off, ignored, floundering and unappreciated.

You may make the assumption that there is something wrong with the individuals and their motivation, or maybe with the circumstances surrounding them – the culture of your organisation. This may or may not be so. But it is more likely that your leadership style is causing the very problem you are complaining about.

The truth of the matter is that no one style of leadership is right for every person or every situation. It's no more appropriate to pride yourself on your unvarying commitment to one style of leadership, than it would be to pride yourself on only ever using your forehand in tennis, or only one iron in golf.

A more productive mindset

There is a simple model of leadership that's been around for many years, which will give you an insight into what's going wrong (when it does), and how to get it right for the future.

Figure 8 shows how it looks.

Figure 8 – Matching your leadership style to the needs of your followers

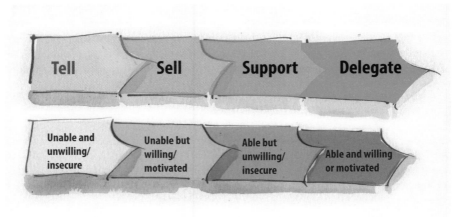

There's a continuum from command and control through to delegation:

- *Telling* (style 1) is traditional command and control. The leader tells people what to do and monitors their work closely before telling them what to do next.
- In *selling* (style 2), you explain the whole task and engage the person in the need to do it, before giving them the jobs they need to do. Ownership of the job still remains with you as leader.
- In *supporting* people (style 3), you include them in ownership of the job and invite their participation in designing and planning solutions.
- When *delegating* (style 4) you give away the whole job to someone, only retaining ultimate accountability for its completion.

So, your leadership style could go from command and control at one end of the continuum, to full delegation, hands-off management, at the other, and it's good to develop the ability to use all the styles. The critical change in mindset needed is that the choice of which style to use should not be dictated by your personal preferences as a leader, but by the needs of one or both of two factors: the *situation* you are in, and the *readiness* of your follower.

The situation

Each of these leadership styles may be appropriate to different situations that you may find yourself in, whatever your organisation. If the building is on fire, for example, you don't get people together in a huddle and discuss and take joint decisions as to the best course of action – you bark orders: 'You, call the fire brigade.' 'You, fetch the extinguisher.' 'I'll get people outside.' The more urgent, dangerous or critical the situation, the more you should veer towards the command and control end of the continuum. Don't try to engage everyone's inspired motivation and commitment. As a leader in these situations you are expected to take control. Provide clear direction and, if necessary, instructions, to get the job done.

On the other end of the spectrum, if you are running a long-term project formed of volunteers from various parts of your organisation where it's critical that they enjoy the process and remain committed to participating, it would be a mistake to impose your authority too obviously, if indeed at all. Volunteers need to feel totally involved and useful when participating in projects, so you might choose a supportive, even delegative style of leadership and give them a great deal more freedom than you would in your everyday leadership style.

Follower readiness

The other factor is how ready your follower is. Readiness in this context is a blend of two factors: their *willingness* and their *ability* to carry out the specific task at hand. If a person is *unwilling*, they are resistant to doing the task for whatever reason, and if they are *unable* to do the task, they lack the necessary skill set. The more unwilling and unable they are, the more your style should move to the left-hand command and control end of the continuum. This gives you a guide as to how to match your leadership style to the readiness of your follower – start where *they* are, not where *you* would prefer to operate from.

Ability

A new employee will by definition be at readiness level 1 in terms of ability, even if they have done the same type of work before. They may be keen – it's a new job, so willingness shouldn't be an issue – but they don't have experience in your *particular* organisation or *your* clients, nor of working with their new colleagues. They are at readiness level 1, whatever you or they would like to think, and will need their hand held for a short period until they start to understand the job better. A close, hands-on style of leadership will be appropriate for at least a few weeks.

This is widely misunderstood, and you may find yourself resisting having to do it: 'I've got better things to do – surely he's a big boy and can find his own way around?' And your new employee, with a lot to prove in their new job, may also resist tight management: 'I'm fine, you can leave me alone to get on with it.' Don't fall for it – this critical early stage of the introduction of a new team member to the job will cause you endless problems further down the line if you don't get it right.

As they grow in the job, you can relax your control, *very gradually* drawing back as they learn different aspects of their job, until, when they are fully trained and competent, you can largely leave them to get on with it (though not completely – see 'Working communication skill no. 10', p140 for notes on one-to-one meetings with your team).

Your assessment of their ability may need to be constantly reassessed and should in fact vary greatly depending on the task you are asking them to carry out. Even a fully competent employee, if given a new task to do, or a task with greatly enlarged scope from what they are used to, will slip back down the ability scale, and may need a bit more support until they've learned the new task and regained their confidence. Hence your puzzlement when an apparently perfectly capable person suddenly seems unwilling to take on a new task, or needs hand-holding in a way you are not used to. If you think carefully, you will find that however capable the person has seemed in the past, it was in another role or on a different task.

Willingness/security

Similarly, people vary in their level of willingness and enthusiasm for the job, and in how confident they feel doing it. They may be very able, but not have a good work ethic – an attitude that translates into a lack of willingness to do the job. They may be less able, but very enthusiastic. And their willingness and level of confidence may vary from day to day or situation to situation. All sorts of situations, from office friction to family problems or illness, may cause a formerly confident and capable employee to slip down the readiness scale, requiring a temporary or more permanent change in your leadership style.

An example:

Jurgen, operations director of a medium-sized business providing furnishing services to clients with company apartments or show houses on new developments, ran a large warehousing operation, sourcing, purchasing and storing all the furniture and fittings needed for the properties they serviced. He had worked for many years with Kim, his purchasing manager, and they had established a working relationship in which Jurgen left Kim alone to get on with it, and Kim, fully competent in her role, was happy to be left to do her job in her own way.

One day, things changed. The company acquired a new warehouse some miles from the first and greatly increased the volume of work it did for its clients. Jurgen promoted Kim to senior purchasing manager and recruited a deputy for her, to be based in the other warehouse.

At the point when I was asked to help, both were unhappy. Kim felt overwhelmed at the greatly increased scope of her role – she had never had to manage anybody before, and all the systems she had set up to deal with one warehouse and the previous volume of work seemed not to be working properly any more.

Jurgen couldn't understand why reliable, calm, competent Kim, who largely got on with her job without bothering him, now suddenly seemed to have questions for him all the time. He had got used to leaving her to it, and resented the time she now took away from the other things he had to do.

He was still managing her by delegating the whole job to her. But in some aspects of her work, she had shifted to a state of under-confidence and insecurity and needed to be walked through these aspects until her ability and confidence levels improved. The mismatch caused huge discomfort for both until they realised what was happening.

Although Jurgen didn't like it, Kim's change in confidence and competence required him to move away from his preferred style of complete delegation, at least for a short time. And his resentment and resistance was damaging their relationship and delaying the moment when Kim would find her feet again.

Four leadership styles

SERGEANT TELL   SAM SELL   SOPHIE SUPPORT   DAN DELEGATE

Flexibility is key

It's important to learn to flex your leadership style to meet the changing needs of your organisational situation and your employees' circumstances. One of the most important qualities of leadership is the ability to choose, and use, a range of leadership styles, even adopting styles that are initially unnatural or uncomfortable for you.

The good news is that if you match your style to a person's current task-specific needs, they will very quickly grow and learn, allowing you to return to a more hands-off mode. You very quickly improve your ability to get work done through your team, and develop individuals through to full ability and willingness – full readiness – in their roles.

How do you apply this mindset to your leadership?

- Practise each style of leadership until you are competent – even if you have a strong preference for one style. You may have to seek out situations, even outside your organisation, to practise all four.
- Recognise that you may have to supervise more tightly at first, whether you like it or not. The less you resist and avoid doing this, the more quickly your employee will grow in confidence and competence, and you can take a step back again.

- Be careful not to flip-flop between style 1 (telling) and style 4 (delegating) – this is confusing and disempowering for people. Move step by step up and down the scale. Just because someone can't be delegated to completely, doesn't mean you have to snatch the work back and do it yourself. A little support may be all they need. Likewise, when they start to show a little competence, don't just disappear. It's like teaching a child to swim – you take your hands off, but keep your eye on them until you're sure they're OK.
- Explain this concept to your team – then you can work together to decide what is the right level of leadership for a given person in a given situation.

Working communication skill no. 10:
holding one-to-one meetings with your
direct reports

The meeting of two personalities is like the contact of two chemical substances: if there is any reaction, both are transformed.

Carl Jung

Do you hold regular one-to-one (1-2-1) meetings with your direct reports? Not just work-in-progress catch-ups, which I expect you do all the time anyway, but real regular one-to-one time with each person who reports directly to you? And if you do, how effective are they?

I often hear comments such as, 'Oh yes, we have regular 1-2-1 meetings because we go to client meetings in the same taxi' or 'There's no need for us to have 1-2-1 meetings in the diary, because we're both in the office at 8 am so we catch up then.' In some organisations the only way to get each other's dedicated attention is to go out for lunch together – both time-consuming and a disaster for your waistline.

Leaders sometimes resist the idea of scheduling 1-2-1s because they feel they're too busy, and the trips in the taxi and the chat at the coffee machine in the morning will do the job. But this is simply not the case.

Regular 1-2-1 meetings set up and conducted properly are an essential management tool and a crucial part of your job. If you manage a team of people, you are responsible both for their work and their welfare. 1-2-1 meetings act as an early warning system because each person who reports to you knows that they will have this regular opportunity to talk to you in private. Have you ever lost a good employee simply because you didn't pick up the warning signs before it was too late? As they begin to trust you and the process, and know that you are committed to the meetings, they will gradually begin to tell you things you need to know that you might not hear otherwise. The 1-2-1 meeting is also the time when you can review their performance and set goals with them. This means that they (and therefore your organisation) are continually moving forward.

Some leaders do recognise that they need to schedule regular 1-2-1 time with members of their team, but are confused about the focus of the meetings. An

>>>

important distinction is that these meetings are for you and your direct report to be working *on* the business rather than *in* the business.

It isn't a formal meeting (no notes need to go on record unless there is a performance improvement issue) and it doesn't require huge follow-up. I recommend that your team member takes any notes needed after you've agreed together what their next steps towards their performance goals should be, and both of you keep a copy of these. This ensures that they own the process and relate to any action steps as their own responsibility. They should record actions, with deadline dates, and the date of your next 1-2-1 meeting (at least monthly).

A simple structure for 1-2-1 meetings

The essential principles:

- Time efficient – a short, 30–40 minute meeting with a clear agenda, to discuss:
  - *How* they are doing: personal news (if any), their behaviour, feelings about the job, anything else they want to share with you.
  - *What* they are doing: progress against their performance objectives (*not* work in progress).
- Frequency – *minimum* is a monthly meeting, weekly or fortnightly for active performance improvement or for a new or insecure person.
- Record – the next step is written down. Deadlines and review times are agreed and in diaries. The next meeting is in the diary.

The process first time you hold the meeting:

1. Explain why you are setting up regular 1-2-1s:
   - To spend time with them to help them improve in their job.
   - Explain the three principles above.
   - To make a regular check on their wellbeing in the job (*how* they are doing).
   - To help them raise their business performance/work on their technical skills (*what* they are doing).
2. *How* they are doing: check their news, their personal wellbeing and how they feel about the job right now. Is there anything they would like to raise with you?

>>>

3. *What* they are doing: review their current performance against their role accountabilities:

- Revisit role accountabilities.
- Agree key measures between you.
- Review performance against last period goals.
- Agree next step SMART objectives with them for each area of accountability.

A typical 1-2-1 meeting record:

- How – how are they; personal news/health issues; any other information.
- What – current performance in the role; good things you have seen/they have done well; progress on goals from last 1-2-1.
- New goals and next steps to be reviewed at next 1-2-1.

Some hints

- The location should be private and the information confidential.
- Be an active listener and ask open questions (see 'Working communication skills nos. 5 and 7,' p61 and 101).
- Let the other person supply answers, come up with solutions and generally do most of the work. Aim for 80:20 talk time, where you do 20 per cent of the talking.
- *Never* cancel 1-2-1 meetings or allow them to be interrupted. One of your primary objectives as a leader is to engage the people in your organisation. Holding these meetings places a premium on time spent with an individual and they will feel valued and engaged. Cancelling and interrupting them sends a negative message.

Conclusion

The whole picture

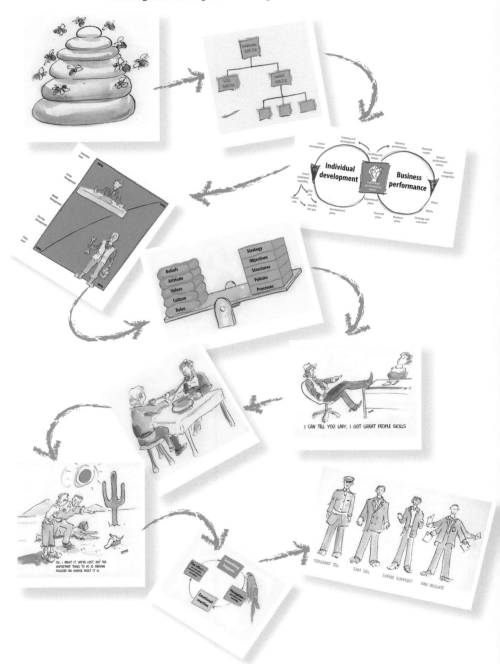

Conclusion – The whole picture

So, this book has brought you on a journey to learn the basics of organisation development as a leader in your own particular hive. Whether you've dipped into it, and are now interested in finding out how it all hangs together, or you have read it from beginning to end and would now like to confirm the shape of that journey for yourself, here's the map:

 Like most people, you start your life in organisations with a focus on yourself as an individual, working for and with other individuals. This view of organisational life gives rise to most of the problems people have in working with each other. One day, though, you have a revelation, an epiphany, and see that there might be another way of looking at it. You see that when people come together, their behaviour is capable of changing and, like a hive of bees, they are capable of working in smooth harmony, to an unseen set of groundrules, for the good of the whole. As an organisational leader, you see that your role now needs to change – though an intrinsic part of this organism, you have a different (not better, or higher) role to play. It is now your job to be a custodian for the growing organism, and to stand slightly away from it, looking with a new detachment for what it needs, and where possible providing it. So you look for gaps, and instead of plugging them yourself, you look for ways to plug them. You look for threats, and instead of riding into battle yourself, you look for ways to support people in fighting and winning the fights they need to fight. And above all you look out for the welfare of everyone in and around the growing organisation, including your own – because, at its best, that's what makes organisational life brilliant.

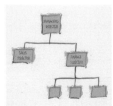 With this new insight about organisations, you see that organisations go through stages of growth, with different issues arising at each stage requiring different responses from their leaders. First generation (1G) organisations pretty much never move beyond being a bunch of individuals responding to market needs on a day-by-day basis and getting it right more by luck than judgement. But after a while working like this stops being fun and exciting. So, with sufficient insight on your part, your organisation moves on to being second generation (2G). Now your role changes to working *on* your organisation instead of *in* it – but this isn't always easy. You gradually find ways of fitting working on the organisation into a working week that still requires you to be one of the worker bees. And this new mindset and change in use of your time slowly start to bring order to your working life and that of the people working around you.

Because *order* is the next area you focus on. You make a conscious move away from the muddle and adrenaline of the early stages. Equally, you recognise that organisational life ruled by checklists, spreadsheets and administrative procedures can quickly throttle the life, creativity and enthusiasm out of people. So you put in, with a light touch, just enough simple structure to smooth the way, and where at all possible encourage people to work with and support each other, rather than finger pointing and pulling against each other. One of your primary tools for achieving this is working with your team members to identify a clear role for each to fulfil in the hive, so that they know exactly what to do to work smoothly and in harmony with no gaps and overlaps.

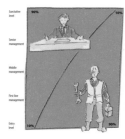

You notice now that you have to make a choice. You started your working life because you were good at something – and that almost certainly wasn't being a manager or a great leader. You had a skill or profession: accountancy, IT skills, making things, repairing things. You were employed initially to exercise this skill, you enjoyed it and you became very good at it. But now your organisation needs you to look after its needs, to become a leader and a manager. The problem in a 2G organisation is that you don't have the luxury of a clear cut-off point between your life as an employee, then as a manager, then as a senior leader. You have to work out for yourself when things change and what characterises the shift from one level to the next. Your working life is pretty much always a mix of all three, and you need to become a master of time management. Your mindset – your attitude to your growing accountability for the organisation and its health – has shifted. And this means that ultimately you have to let go of doing the very thing that you came into organisational life to do, and at a time in your life when it's hard to become a novice again and learn a whole new set of skills. The hive needs a beekeeper more than it needs another bee. It is a choice, and you and those around you will be happier if you recognise that you are not cut out for it, or simply don't want to make it. If you step back, someone who *is* cut out to be a beekeeper will be able to show up.

Let's say you make the choice to move into leadership. You stop getting your sleeves rolled up and getting stuck in whenever there's an issue that might benefit from your original expertise – the bees will never become good at their jobs if you keep doing this. You stand back from the day-to-day work and start to look for where the organisation needs tweaking or needs help from you. The first thing you notice is that everything you notice and its solution seems to have a structural or concrete element – problems with a team member? Reshuffle the team. Complaints about client service? Issue new guidelines. Confusion among employees about direction? Publish the strategy. You are using your original set of (technical) skills to resolve problems, and these solutions don't work. Gradually you realise that issues with and between people need a different type of solution, one which involves a more authentic and intimate process of exploring their concerns, listening to their ideas and allowing them to implement their own solutions in their own way – each knows their job in the hive and they have their own wisdom, if you will just listen to it. The solutions take longer, but tend to stick. You learn to manage the balance between concrete problems needing concrete solutions and more subtle problems needing a more nuanced approach.

I CAN TELL YOU LADY, I GOT GREAT PEOPLE SKILLS

Now you realise that your growing accountability for the organisation has led you to question your relationship with the people you work with. You feel somehow distanced from them, and the ways you used to communicate with them don't seem to work so well now that your role has changed. You may even struggle with a feeling that you are no longer one of the swarm. You start to explore how to communicate with others so they understand clearly what you require of them, respond clearly and unequivocally and do what's needed. You realise that everyday social skills aren't a precise enough tool to achieve this, and you learn to be more careful about what you say and how you speak to others. Equally you realise that simple social skills aren't sufficient for others in your team to work effectively with each other, and you start to train them too. Eventually you all draw a distinction between getting on together socially, and working effectively together, and you find that, far from damaging your mutual enjoyment in work, this distinction enhances it. There are fewer misunderstandings and mistakes and less chit-chat at work, while those who want to, including you, can relax completely in social settings and simply enjoy one another's company.

This leads you to a growing realisation that you can actually set the tone for your organisation and its culture. Rejecting society's prevailing culture of individualism, finger pointing and blame and learning to work effectively and support each other you build a new culture of true partnership at work – you become a hive, with an equally essential and valued role for everyone. You come to work with your focus on how you can make working life more successful and enjoyable for every member of your team, and they each come to work looking to help and support each other – and you – to be successful. Creating a culture of partnership at work is one of your key tasks as a leader; you do and provide anything that's necessary to have it thrive.

One of the foundations of this culture is a new, unfamiliar and refreshing attitude to accountability at work (and for many of you, out of it too). Everything works better if people promise what they can realistically achieve, give clear deadlines and, as far as humanly possible, meet those deadlines. And if one of you fails, it works much better if you put your energy not into blaming and making excuses, but into working out why you failed and putting measures in place to make sure that, within reason, you won't fail again. You all learn to make clear unambiguous requests and simple clear responses, and cut out the waffle, fudging and wriggling that wastes everybody's time and tries their patience.

You become more self-aware as you explore these new ways of communicating, and you realise that your actions are not always driven by the more enlightened 'you'. Instead you become aware of a small inner voice, like a parrot on your shoulder whispering in your ear, that sometimes causes you to fail, to react inappropriately or to avoid accountability when you know your role is to step up to it. The more you become interested in and aware of this small voice, the more you find you can make choices about what it's saying to you. You find this frees you to step up and be brave more and more often. You use your new-found insight to give feedback to and coach others, and they learn to manage themselves more effectively too.

And finally you learn as you come into contact with more and more people and different situations that there are many ways of being a leader. It's not about you and your preferences and natural leadership style, but what your organisation and the people in it need in any given set of circumstances. You stay in touch with people by meeting and coaching them individually, but you manage them as a constantly moving and dynamic organism.

And as you challenge your mindsets and learn the skills, sharing them with others so they become 'just the way we do things around here', you find that your organisation ceases to need all your energy and attention. It and the people who work in it have internalised the wisdom needed to become self-sustaining. The organisation really has acquired a life of its own, and while you have a role in its ongoing health and success, it has ceased to be entirely dependent on you – and it's brilliant. You have acquired a whole new set of insights and skills. You are a fully developed beekeeper – a custodian for this organisation and its bees, and maybe for others you may move to or choose to set up in the future.

Your job is done – well done indeed.

Leaders Lab

Amanda Baines and Kate Mercer

With the establishment of Leaders Lab in 2013, Kate and Amanda combined their many years of expertise in business consultancy and coaching with their shared belief in building healthy organisations that encourage teams and individuals to shine. Their practical and accessible approach produces a durable and sustainable organisation that inspires people and supports them in achieving outstanding results.

At Leaders Lab Kate and Amanda work with leaders who, while they run successful, expert businesses, sometimes struggle to find the time and expertise to really engage their staff and gain the full commitment and accountability of everyone who works in the organisation.

They specialise in leadership, team and organisation development, as well as delivering executive coaching on a one-to-one level. Business leaders and their staff develop the skills they need to do their job well, gain clarity about their accountabilities and develop powerful action plans to achieve their goals. Leaders Lab enables businesses to create powerful leadership, stable and durable roles, effective communication and workable processes for the next phase of their growth.

www.leaderslab.co.uk

+44 1865 881056